Tommy Franks, Ph.D.

Born To Win

A Winner's Destiny

All rights reserved under International Copyright Law.
International Standard Book Number-10: 0-926044-01-X
International Standard Book Number-13: 978-0-926044-01-2
Library of Congress number: 9780926044012

Unless otherwise indicated, all Scripture quotations are taken from the
King James Version of the Bible.

Due to the Author's prerogative, some words are in small letters and
some are capitalized for clarity and emphasis and not necessarily in
accordance with standard grammatical practice.

Unless otherwise stated, whenever the masculine gender is used, it
applies to both men and women.

First Edition 2009.

To order additional copies, please contact us.
BookSurge
www.booksurge.com
1-866-308-6235
orders@booksurge.com

DEDICATION

I dedicate this book **_Born to Win: A Winner's Destiny_** to my wife Karen, children, family, friends, and all of you who read this book.

CONTENTS

FORWARD

Dr. Tommy Franks' new book **Born to Win: A Winner's Destiny** presents the reader with many wonderful and exciting opportunities to alter their thinking and lifestyle in order to live more productively, positively, and meaningfully. The Lord has provided each one of us with a multitude of unique gifts, talents, and abilities. None of us should live our lives in fear, poverty, hopelessness, want, or insignificance. This book shows us how to live a fuller and deeper life in the Lord and how to walk with purpose, passion, and confidence.

In a world filled with a multitude of legitimate concerns and tremendous problems, we need to hear voices of hope, encouragement, and success. We need coaches and cheerleaders. We all need to know that we can be winners in this life and not losers, to be productive instead of being unproductive, and make a big difference in others lives instead of making a little difference. Loving, giving, caring, sharing and a host of other positive attributes enrich our lives and give them meaning and value. This book shows us how to move from a position of weakness and defeat to strength and success.

Dr. Franks is a wonderful and enthusiastic leader, teacher, and servant at All Saints' Episcopal Church in downtown Lakeland, Florida. He has a deep love for the Lord and a wonderful knowledge of the Bible along with a great passion to help people succeed in life. He ardently desires that all who read this book prosper and grow as human beings who are made in the image and likeness of God. His heartfelt sincerity and enthusiasm about prosperous and godly living shines from page to page.

Enjoy the book and may your life always be filled with God's grace and riches.

The Rev. Reid Hensarling
Associate Rector of All Saints' Episcopal Church
Lakeland, Florida

INTRODUCTION

YOU and I were born to WIN! Nowhere in our universe does it say that you are a loser. The Bible says that you are "The Apple of God's Eye". God has made you to ride upon the high places of the earth. You deserve the very BEST that our Father has to offer. He wants you to be a "Winner" and to have an abundant life filled with joy. He wants YOU to be happy, healthy, and wise. YOU are the BEST product that the Father has ever produced! You were created in His image and in His class. As a Winner, you expect to win!

Galileo said, "You cannot teach a man anything. You can only help him discover it within himself."

Each human being is born as a brand new creation...someone who has never existed before...with the capacity to win in life...each person having a unique way of seeing, hearing, touching, tasting, thinking, and doing things. Each has her own unique potentials, capabilities, and limitations. Each is a significant and creative being...creation of God... a real winner. Most people are not 100% winners or 100% losers. We all have "bad hair" days. I have no hair...So, as you can see, I have seen a few bad hair days in times past. However, once a person is on the road to winning, her chances of continuing to win in the game of life are pretty good. Winners have different potentials. Winners do their own thinking. They think for themselves. Winners never play the "helpless" game...nor do they play the "blame" game. They play to win. They assume responsibility for their own lives. Winners are able to love and be loved. Winners have a zest and passion for life. They have energy! They have passion for the things in which they believe. Winners care about the world, the earth, and the environment. They are not isolated from the general concerns of society, but they are concerned and compassionate about improving the quality of life. Winners want to make the world a better place and enjoy life to its fullest!

You are the only you. There will never be another exact you!

chapter

ONE

Born to Win

You were born to win. You were born to succeed. Success is yours in accordance with the Holy Scriptures. God wants you to be a winner in this life...not a failure. God has given you the power to have anything you desire. God owns it all and He wants to share His wealth and resources with you...and your family.

As winners, we need to see ourselves as God sees us... successful, whole, full of faith, bold, and "more than conquerors". YOU have the POWER of God within you. You have God the Father, His Son, and the Holy Spirit. God wants you to be a winner in life; however, He leaves the choice up to you. He will not force you to be a winner. He will not force His "winning attitude" upon you. Winning comes from within.

The Gospel says a lot about winning. The Gospel EXCITES me because it talks about life on Planet Earth and the life to come hereafter. Our destiny is to win. Our destiny is Planet Heaven. Our destiny is the throne room. We will reign with Christ forever. We were created to win. God loves us so much that He allowed His only Son to die so that we could live and be successful, HEALTHY, and full of great joy. I do not think that anyone intentionally wants to be a loser. No one gets up in the morning and says, "Today, I think I will be a loser. I was born to lose. I'm a nincompoop. I am a complete loser!"

As Winners, we are on a Divine Assignment by Divine Appointment by a Divine Authority...everyday while on Planet Earth. We are filled with God's Spirit and His dynamic ability. Our purpose is to make a difference for Christ in our communities, churches, schools, cities, and nation.

Success will come to us as we accept our responsibility in the Kingdom of God. Think about this: You are the only person in this world that can stop you from God's best and God's success. GOD is for YOU. He is not against you. He has given you abundant life...now in this life. God has made you a winner! (Mt.17, Ps.17, 56, 59, 62, 118, Deut.32, Jn.10, Mk.10).

WINNERS have plans. LOSERS have excuses. WINNERS find the answer. LOSERS seek out the problem. WINNERS are part of the answer. LOSERS are normally the problem. WINNERS say that it is highly possible. LOSERS say that it is definitely impossible. Losers are complainers and whiners.

As a winner, the following do not belong to you:
- FAILURE (Phil.4:13)
- POVERTY (Phil.4:19)
- FEAR (2 Tim.1:7)
- DOUBT (Rom.12:3)
- WEAKNESS (Ps.27:1, Dan.11:32)
- DEFEAT (2 Cor.2:14)
- IGNORANCE (1 Cor.1:30)
- SIN (1 Jn.1:7)
- WORRY (1 Pet.5:7)
- BONDAGE (2 Cor.3:17)
- CONDEMNATION (Rom.8:1).

We all instinctively categorize everyone we meet (including ourselves) as Winners or Losers. We may not necessarily share our opinions with others, but we still judge people...good, bad, indifferent, we all do it from time to time. We also judge things. Good judgment is not a bad thing; however, judging people without knowing them is not a good thing. Whether we admit it or not, we all judge. Sometimes, we pretend that we are only inquisitive...while all the while we are placing judgment on a person or group of people. "Judge not that you be not judged."

Furthermore, as you are blessed as a Winner, you will have an APPRECIATION for others and a POSITIVE ATTITUDE. You will make commitments and have good communication with others. You will have a greater LOVE, SENSITIVITY, and COMPASSION for others. Your SENSE of HUMOR, PATIENCE, and TOLERANCE for the weaknesses in others will expand. Regardless of where you are in your earthly walk with God, being a winner will make you feel good about yourself. You will begin to expand your goals and your horizons. You will invest in your mind and spirit by studying the WORD, good positive books, CDs, and DVDs. Attending Church will be very important to you. You will spend quality time with quality people. You will use your time wisely and you will be TEACHABLE.

YOU were created to be a "Winner". YOU were made for GREATNESS. You were made to soar like an eagle...not like a chicken in the barnyard eating chicken feed with the hogs. YOU were made for excellence. Winning is now part of your life. YOU were made to rule and reign with Christ while on earth...and later in heaven.

"And YOU shall eat in PLENTY and be SATISFIED. You have become a winner because you belong to the family of God. Abundance is YOURS. You will not lack. The Lord is your Shepherd. God has been GOOD to you. He will never let you down. You will never be put to shame (Rom.10:11). God loves you so much. You were born to win!

IT'S IMPOSSIBLE
By Tommy Franks, Ph.D.

It's impossible for the sun to stop shining.
It's impossible for the moon to stop reflecting.
It's impossible for the oceans to dry up.
It's impossible for the wind to stop blowing.
It's impossible for a little baby not to cry.
It's impossible for the singing birds not to fly.
It's just impossible for the world to stop turning.
It's simply impossible for us to live without God's love
    and care...
And kindness, and the little things that
He does for us because He loves us!

It's impossible for the time to go backwards.
It's just impossible for Him not to love us and think of us
    continuously.
It's impossible for us to go on without Him.
It's impossible not to get excited when we hear His
    voice.
It's impossible for us not to love Him.
It's just impossible for us to think of a world without Him.
Why? I wish I could completely explain it,
But that too is just impossible.
All I know is: God loves you and me with all His heart.
It's just impossible for Him to deny His children.

chapter

TWO

Success Is Yours

I am so excited for you. You have such incredible potential before you. You want to be a winner and you shall be. Our loving Father has made you a Winner. You do not follow the crowd. The crowd follows you. Many are now asking questions about your success in life and your achievements. You have resources that the world would love to possess. You refuse mediocrity. You refuse to be a loser! You refuse to be bound by circumstances. You have faith in God and in yourself. You are on a mission to win. God has given you the Kingdom. As you put your trust in Him, you cannot lose. SUCCESS is yours. You are the victor. The kingdom of light will prevail in your life. The Bible says that "You are the salt and light of the earth".

You and I are in God's class. He made us in His image. You and I are members of the highest social order and class on this earth and in heaven. We are in God's Class. You were made in His direct image. His fingerprints are all over you. His DNA is inside you. He created you in His image. You are in the same CLASS as God. You are not God, but you are His child. You were made in His image. God will live forever...and so will you! As a child of God, you will live forever in heaven. You now have "family status" with God. You are bone of His Bone...flesh of His Flesh...body of His Body, and the Blood of Jesus Christ His Son flows through your veins. When God looks at YOU, He looks on the inside, not on the surface. God sees the real BEAUTY in YOU. He sees a true WINNER.

Be strong. Live long. YOU and I are winners who bring success to our communities. Think about this...Jesus was... is...and will always be a Winner indeed because He brought us abundant living and revival by destroying disease, infirmities, pains, sickness, poverty, and death. He literally brought heaven to earth.

The choice to be a winner is ours. Jesus has given us a positive mental, spiritual, and physical attitude...if we choose to accept it. No longer do we have to be average. No longer do we have to be in debt over our heads. Jesus said that we could be "free indeed". However, the CHOICE is OURS. Jesus brought us abundant resources. He has given us back our dignity, self-esteem, and righteousness (right standing with God). He has given us the Holy Spirit to comfort and ASSIST us at all times. He has done all of this...just for you, me, and all who will accept Him. Oh, the mercy of the Lord is so great and everlasting. He has set us FREE indeed!

We can see the salvation of the Lord. We do NOT have to fear. God is with us. The battle is not ours, but His. We cast ALL our cares, debts, anxieties, and reservations upon Him. He will smite and destroy the enemy before our face. If we are obedient, we shall eat the fat of the land. No good thing will He withhold from us because we are His children. He is our Father. There is not one good thing that He will withhold from us. He wants you to be truly happy.

We were born for such a time as this. We were born to be successful. We are destined for GREATNESS and the throne...which Christ will share with us. We are destined to rule and reign forever. We are WINNERS. If God be for us, who can be against us? Life is so SWEET. We have more POWER locked up within us right now than we will ever need. The Greater One lives within. He is all powerful and will put us over. We go forth in courage and faith.

You determine your own Success. You were made for success, but your destiny is in your hands and God's. You can choose to be a winner or not. The choice is yours. Success wants to be a part of your life. You were born to be a Winner! You can now go forth CHARGED in the POWER and AUTHORITY of God. His ability is yours. Your very words are filled with faith, success, love, mercy, compassion, and energy. People now come to you for answers. You speak forth the vision and Word of God. You give and it is given back to you in abundance. Blessings are yours because of your obedience in giving. You have given and now the harvest is coming back to you because God's Word says, "While the earth remains, seedtime and harvest, and cold and heat, and summer and winter, and day and night shall not cease" (Gen.8:22). Being in the Winner's Circle is a lifestyle for YOU. It is not a chore, job, or sacrifice, but a lifestyle...abundant living lifestyle.

You are a POWERFUL winning force on this earth. You have become a channel of God's blessings to others. Success is yours.

What we did in out past is gone. Does our past have to repeat itself? No. NO. Look at the life of Abraham Lincoln. He was a miserable failure for the first fifty years of his life. He failed at almost everything he did up until the time he was elected President of America. What happened to him? Well, for one thing he got tired of losing. Did Honest Abe have a winning behavior? Incredibly so! Did he recognize what it would take to experience a winning performance? Yes! Was he successful? Does the sun shine in Florida? Does it snow in Canada? Absolutely! President Lincoln went on to become...perhaps our greatest President ever. He got tired of losing and decided to start winning...not only for himself, but also for all of Americans.

Someone once said, "Show me a GOOD loser...and I will show you a loser!" I believe that when the student is ready, the teacher will come. I do not believe that we necessarily learn more from failure than we do from success or winning. However, I do believe that there is a healthy balance between the two. To know victory is ecstatic. To know victory is impressive. It is thrilling, tingling, rapturous, delightful, pleasurable, and truly exciting! To know defeat is normally a sad thing to experience. Why? Because we are NOT built to lose. We are NOT meant to be losers. Man is born to win. Period! As I stated earlier, we are born to win. Therefore today, let us go forth with the following thoughts: As a Winner, I have a winning attitude, behavior, and a winning performance. This creates success. Our past does not dictate our future. We live in the present, but we plan for the future. Our future will be better than our past.

Some people are looking for success everywhere... except in the right place. Success is within you. That's right. The beautiful TREASURE of SUCCESS is on the inside of you. Believe it. It only needs to be uncovered and discovered... released and set free. Marvelous! Look inside. See what you were meant to be and see...faith in God, wisdom, purpose, goodness, goals, your destiny, your finest hour that is about to begin...the start of a brand new you. We all want PURPOSE in our lives. We want IDENTITY. We want SECURITY. We want ACCEPTANCE. We want WISDOM. We can have it all if we choose. The choice is ours.

You were created for a purpose. You were designed for greatness. Every atom and cell in your human body cries out for success. You think like a Winner. No one is ever born to lose. Yes, I know about the song "Born To Lose" by Ray Charles. I remember being stationed at Laon AFB, France in 1966...and listening to that song almost daily. It had a "catchy" tune. I would sing along with Ray. I would confess the saying, "Born to Lose"...and eventually I became a loser...a real loser.

No reflection on Ray Charles, but the words and gist of the song are NOT true. We are NOT born to lose. We are born to win, to have style, class, flair, expression, and success. No person on earth is created to lose. We were made to be productive and fruitful. We have goals and aspirations to excel. We are not afraid to venture out into the deep. Sometimes, it may be a little risky, but we persevere. We continue even when others have given up on us. We are not afraid of failure. We do not think defeat. It is not part of our vocabulary. We plunge into the task at hand...and know that eventually...if we stick with it, we will be successful.

How you view yourself is "where it's happening". That's real. How others see you may not be true or factual. The good treasure is down inside you. It wants to surface. It wants to be free to blossom and bring forth a rich aroma of fragrance as a savory bouquet. It has been there since conception. Some people take it to the grave with them without ever releasing it. This...my friend...is tragic. You were born for success. You were born to WIN and keep on Winning by using the treasure that was given to you by God...as talents, ability, skills, warmth, and personality.

Success takes teamwork: Working together for a common goal or purpose and enthusiasm with outstanding results. Incredible Teamwork consists of boundless enthusiasm, energy, and dedication.

Someone once said, "When we are ready...the teacher will appear."

Winners (people of success) realize that they are persons of great worth. They have class. They have style. They are children of great destiny. They have seeds of greatness down inside them. These seeds of greatness will germinate and grow to the surface and become a great harvest! Then they will grow to maturity and blossom out and bear much fruit...

Winners will find a way to get it done. They will say, "I'm going to do it"...and then do it. Winners of Destiny have DREAMS, VISIONS, and DESIRES. They have a responsibility. They are already a "somebody". They don't have to try to be a "somebody". They are children of destiny who refuse mediocrity. Winners decide the right way...what is fair to all and then do it.

I keep telling myself, "I'm going to do it. Self, you are unique. Out of 9.2 billion people who have lived on this earth for the last 6,000 years, you are the only you. There is no one else like you. There never has been. There never will be. Therefore, Self, take your PLACE. Do what you were designed to do. Never take a back seat to mediocrity or apathy. Follow your DREAM. Follow your goals. Build upon your successes. Yes, temporary set-backs will come, but they are just that...temporary. The real you is a winner and will take nothing less than the best. Therefore, today...Self, you will make it. You will make things happen. You've decided to move forward because you have confidence in yourself. You have confidence in your talents and abilities. You refuse to give up. Self, you will make it and you will make it happen for others too. PERIOD!"

Winners know that they can do it. Success is theirs because they have character. They have inherited characteristics of strength. They are free from inferiority, self-consciousness, weakness, and detrimental habits. They are free moral agents who make good sensible and intelligent decisions that will profit this world, others, and their communities. Winners affect change, people, and things in a positive way. Winners are instruments of change. They posture themselves with a sense of humor, zeal, active performance, and a lot of smiles. They choose to like people. They choose to have fun and be happy. Happy people are 25 to 30% more productive than unhappy people. Happy people are healthier people and they live longer.

Someone said, "I may not be able to change the whole world around me, but I CAN CHANGE the WAY I see the world within me."

Winners of Destiny find worthwhile work and then do it, not lackadaisically or half heartedly, but professionally and energetically. They know that their work is important. They make the world a better place in which to live. They know that they are making a difference. They know how to work together with a common bond to get things done. Winners value others. They are results oriented. They display sound values that guide their plans, decisions, and actions in a positive forward movement. Winners know that they are needed. They are in control of their own destiny and goals.

Winners respect others. They want to do the right thing and they want things done the right way. They have enthusiasm. They encourage others. When a real winner walks into a room to encourage someone, it's like throwing gasoline on a spark. An explosion of energy takes place. We all need to have the approval of others. This is a basic need in every human being on Planet Earth. We need to know that we are valuable, accepted, worthy, creditable, needed, and loved. Therefore, let us encourage others and give them hope and support.

For centuries, "He who had the gold made the rules". That does not work anymore on a permanent basis. Some of the possessors of the gold have gone blind from the glare of their own self-brilliance and self-importance.

In this book "Born to Win: A Winner's Destiny", you will realize one thing: Nothing (not one iota) is going to change unless you take a stand as a team player and implement change. Change is inevitable and necessary...and sometimes very difficult. Change requires us to stretch sometimes. Sometimes change is necessary to get what we want out of life on a consistent basis. We can change frustration or disappointment into personal power and influence. How? FOCUS on what our hearts really desire. We must change.

We can change how we feel...and be happy, joyful, and even energetic. We can have better relationships, more money, and a better quality of life. How? We must truly have a desire to be happy, a desire to feel better, and want positive changes that will bring about these kinds of essentials. Once, we make up our minds to change for the better, incredible things begin to fall in place. We begin to change our mental focus. We begin to pay attention to our words, our thoughts, our present state, and our future. Sometimes, radical change may be the answer.

We can take charge of our own lives and create the types of feelings and passion that we truly want in life. You see, our emotions are created by motion. We create our emotions and feelings by motion...by what we do with our bodies...minds...our movements, thoughts, and even our gestures. We are responsible for our own state of mind. Once you realize that you have this kind of power within you, you begin to take charge of your life. You begin to use this ability. You begin to have more fun, joy, passion, and energy than you ever dreamed possible. You begin to smile more. You become aware that if you can control your face with a smile, you will control your state of mind

Now, let us get back to FOCUS. What we focus on determines how we feel. How we feel determines how we behave. How we behave determines our success. Our success determines our future. Our future determines our Winner's Destiny. You and I deserve the very best in life...and may we always have it.

BOTTOMLINE: Success is yours. Winning is your way of life. You have experienced victory after victory. Remind yourself of those victories often. You are the best "you" that will ever be. No one can ever produce a better "you" than you...no one. You have identified the talent that lies within "you" and your treasured diamond potential. You are now using it as fully as possible toward a purpose and plan. This makes you feel good about yourself and worthwhile because...at the same time, you are also benefiting others. This, my friend, is success and truly "winning" at the game of life.

chapter

THREE

Be Persistent

Calvin Coolidge once said, "Nothing in the world can take the place of persistence. Talent will not; nothing is more common than unsuccessful men or women with talent. Genius will not; un-rewarded genius is almost a proverb. Education will not; the world is full of educated derelicts…"

Winning in life, we must be persistent. Winning is rooted in our inner man…self…inner being. The outer trappings may be wonderful; however, our happiness and joy are created from within…not the other way around. Many rich men or women would love to have inner peace without inner conflict. Are they successful? Sometimes, they are. But that is not the type of success in which I am referring. I believe we can have both. It is not either...or. I believe we can certainly have "things"..."outward manifestations of wealth"...and also have the inner peace that comes with "high morals, family values, consideration for others, benevolence, and old fashioned integrity". Call me old fashioned. That's okay. I believe that we can be successful internally and externally...if we are persistent. God has never made a "nobody" and never will. He created you in His likeness.

You as a winner...were born with an infinite value system. As you matured, you also developed your own values. You began to see yourself as valuable with great worth. You began to see yourself as you were created to be. You began to see yourself with almost "limitless" potential. As a person of priceless value, significance, and importance, you soon realized that you did not have to do anything that encroached upon your conscience and sense of ethics. You began to choose your own goals, lifestyle, occupation, and relationships. Society no longer dictated your destiny. You did. No one could continue to dominate, intimidate, or manipulate you. You became responsible for your own actions. You became a tremendous winner with a winning attitude. Everyday is a new challenge. Everyday is a new opportunity. Everyday is a new juncture of excitement. Everyday is a new adventure. You can hardly wait until tomorrow! As you treat others with dignity and respect, you will be treated in kind. Life is good. If you sow good things, good words, and good seeds into the lives of others, a great harvest will also come to you.

Will we ever experience failure? Yes, but only on a temporary basis. Failure does not have to be permanent. Will failure stop us? No. We will get up and "keep on trucking". We will be persistent and use failure as a type of fertilizer for natural growth. Failure can benefit us only if we allow our-selves to learn something from it and perhaps...change...if necessary.

As a Winner, you create an atmosphere for success. You focus on the important items at hand...not mundane idio-syncrasies or quirks that will mean nothing a hundred years from now. Think about it: One Hundred Years from now, will these small things make any difference? No. The important thing is to: Believe in God, your family, others, your country, and yourself. Continue to believe in the strengths, abilities, and talents that lie within you. Believe that you and God control your destiny and not those around you or nega-tive circumstances. Within you lies the power to be a major influence on the world and those around you. As a Winner, you do not believe in happenstance or flukes. You believe that things happen in Divine order and with a purpose. You know where you have been and more importantly, where you are going. And that excites you on life. It sets you on fire to be a flame and to be high on life.

You were not made "second class". You were cre-ated "first class" to ride the high places. You were made for incredible greatness. Continue to think big. Continue to be persistent. No one can make you feel inferior or intimidate you without your permission. You have become a caring person. You have become a loving person. "Hate" or "prej-udice" has no place in your heart because goodness and warmth are there. Winners love all people because they know that we are all one human race and in some way related to each other. We all came from Adam and Eve... no exceptions.

We do not compare ourselves with others or what others have accomplished. We do not try to be like the "Jones'" or the "Smiths'". Even though we have heroes in whom we have learned much, we march to the beat of our own drum orchestrated by our loving Father. We have distinguished ourselves as a people of action and productivity. We have sown seeds. The seeds have come up...First the blade, then the ear, and then the corn. A tremendous and bountiful harvest is all around us. We have more than enough.

Sometimes, an unlearned person who does not know you very well...may say, "You will not make it. You do not have what it takes to be successful. You just don't have what it takes to be a winner. Forget it. You will always be mediocre. You are a nobody." But you don't listen to her. You continue to persevere. You continue to hurdle every type of obstacle...even when some of your friends offer nothing but discouragement. You are tenacious. You have a made up mind. You are persistent. You win.

Your heart is not "in the quitting mode" because you will never leave a sinking ship. You will bail the water out. You will repair the damage and continue on course. You will make it to Treasure Island. Treasure Island is a fun place to drink suds in the warm sun and sand. You will enjoy the palm trees and coconut trees. The weather there is mild and gentle with the warm breeze like honey blowing through your silky, fine hair. You will make it to the island and find the treasure. The golden treasure will make you rich beyond measure. The treasure will be sweet and enchanting with incredible wealth. Riches belong to you.

Your positive attitude, team spirit, and friendly hospitality have made you a Winner! Where are those who opposed you? People now attempt to emulate and imitate you. You smile and hold out your hand to assist them...because as a Winner, you never hold a grudge. You forgive and move forward. You pray for those who have hurt you. Your standards and goals are extremely high. You have high class. You have finesse, refinement, and confidence. Your self-esteem is high. Why? Because you know that your future is in God's Hands and that your future is brighter than your past!

Many times in life, it is NOT so much what happens to us as much as it is "how we handle what happens to us". Many times, it is the way we look at something or view it. How do we respond to it? Do we get over anxious or go "crazy" about the small things? Life is not always a bowl of cherries. Even though life is fun, exciting, filled with continuous opportunities and wonderful events to enjoy…life still has its peculiarities, ambiguities, and challenges. Some of us grew up watching Jiminy the Cricket (Walt Disney cartoon character) on TV. He was the type of animated character that was always positive and urging individuals to follow their conscience and dreams. He was committed to "seeking the truth" and "never giving up" on goals. He wanted others to succeed! He wanted people to be healthy and wealthy. Not once did I ever hear him talk about what he wanted. He was always talking to others about their good qualities, rich talents, various abilities, and "giving them encouragement and motivation". He knew about Winning.

Today, in our society, basically there are two types of individuals…Givers and takers. Givers will always win. Period! Takers seem to think: "If I will just be smart enough, tough enough, ambitious enough, lucky enough, and take enough…life will be good to me. I will make it. I will excel. I will be admired." I will…Blah, Blah, Blah. That never happens. Takers are losers…BIG losers.

True winners know better. They "make it happen for others". They know that if they plant enough seeds into other people's lives, that a harvest will come up and they will share in the harvest at some point in time. We all desire to be winners. We believe in living life to its fullest…gusto. We are destined to be successful. What goes around comes around. Success is not just the destination; it's also the journey along the way. Some believe that we can quantify success by the amount of money we make…not necessarily so.

Mother Teresa would argue with us on that point. She did great exploits with almost nothing except the "love and compassion" in her heart and the work of her small frail hands. If money was the only measuring stick, why do we have so many unhappy and discontented millionaires and wealthy people? Success is not measured by what we purchase or produce. Success is what we feel inside about ourselves. How do we feel about ourselves? We will project on the outside what we feel on the inside.

chapter

FOUR

Winners Want Action

Once upon a time, success (being a winner) was measured by good old fashioned, traditional values, morals, and Christian principles...like truth, morality, integrity, a kind heart, rightness, and good solid virtues. I have a little secret that I want to share with you. This secret has stood the test of time. Success is still measured by the same traditional values of yester-year. The opposite is called "self-gratification" which is for losers pretending to be temporary winners. Every human being can be a winner...no exceptions. We may not always feel like winners or look like winners, but we can be. We may not always look like we are winning, but we can. Many losers are potential "winners" in disguise. Oh yes! I was one of them until I found out who I was.

In today's society, winners want action. They ask questions. They educate themselves. If we do not ask questions, we do not receive answers. Sometimes, we need clarification on things. Sometimes, we need to ask for a raise or a new position that is becoming available. If we purchase an item at a department store and it turns out to be a lemon or an inferior product, winners go to the store manager or owner and request a full refund or exchange. However, the non-winner complains and whines, but does not even bother to challenge or ask the proprietor for her money back...even when the guarantee is in writing. This type of non-challenging episode is a lose/lose situation. The business loses because of the adverse publicity and the customer loses because he has accepted an inferior or broken product.

Winners want action. They educate themselves! They become educated consumers. They are not afraid to take something back to the store. Receipts are kept in a safe place...just for this purpose. Winners have no time to agonize over a problem. They get up...get going...get action. They do not "sweat the small stuff". Obstacles do not become millstones or a deterrent to the winner. Solving problems or removing an obstacle is a winner's way of life. Winners work at accomplishments. They meet challenges "head-on". They do not take "no" for an answer. The word "no" only spurs them on to success. Winners believe. Winners persevere. Winners are persistent. They believe that "all things are possible". They believe in a Higher Power...God. They believe in themselves, their families, in others, and this wonderful world of ours. Is our world perfect? Absolutely not. But will whining and bad-mouthing our society make it better? No.

Obstacles become "stepping stones" to the winner. Winners look for the rainbow and the pot of gold. A couple of years ago, I saw a double rainbow near Tucson, Arizona. I thought I had died and gone to heaven. It was one of the most beautiful scenes and sites that I have ever experienced in my whole life. Almost the entire sky was dark blue. The sun was peeking between two huge clouds. Brilliant rainbow colors sparkled across the horizon. I felt exhilarated and ecstatic. I felt like a kid in a brand new candy store. That was the first and only double rainbow that I have ever seen...But I'm sure there will be others.

Contrariwise, losers complain about the rain...even though yesterday, they were complaining about the drought. Winners are persistent souls. They will not "give up". Defeat is not in their vocabularies. For the winner, "failure" is another way NOT to do something. They learn from failures. They do not embrace failure, but they embrace the learning process and experience from the failure. Sometimes, even when they are told that they "don't have what it takes", winners take it with stride...like water rolling off a duck's back. Winners do NOT go backwards. That is indeed non-productive.

Napoleon Bonaparte, after crossing the English Channel...burned all of the ships behind him. He and his men had to go forward. They could not go back. They had to win the war. They did.

Another good trait of winners is: They know there is plenty of room at the top. They focus on improving their own abilities and attributes rather than putting someone else down or hurting another's forward progress. When a winner enters a room, she doesn't have to say a word. Winners know who they are. They come with a "presence". They come with dignity. They respect themselves and they respect others. They truly believe: Do it for others and they will do it for you. Winners are not afraid to ask for help when necessary. This does not lessen their character, worth, qualities, or self-esteem. They are humble men/women; therefore, seeking help or counsel from others who know more is not a "drawback" for them, rather an excellent quality. Go forth...today...as a winner. You have the power to influence the world.

Winners and successful people outlast tough times and recessions. They never see themselves losing. If you think you will fail, you will. If you think a situation is hopeless, it probably is. There is an infallible statement that the Master Teacher (Jesus) once made, "Nothing shall be impossible unto you". Who was He talking about? He was talking about those that have faith and truly believe in themselves and God. You see, even the Carpenter had great faith in Himself and the Creator of the Universe. He knew His purpose, His mission, His abilities, and His eternal destiny. Difficult times are only temporary. You are NOT. You are eternal.

Winners keep on going in good times, bad times, sad times, hard times, and stormy times. Adversity becomes a challenge. The only thing that can stop a winner is himself or herself. Winners are not born. They are made. They come in all kinds of packages...small, large, short, tall, black, white, brown, red, and yellow. Experience, education, intelligence, money, and talent are not prerequisites. Winning is a deliberate decision. It comes from the inside out. As human beings, we are born to win; however, a decision must be made to be a winner. That decision can come early in life, mid-life, or late in life.

The Kentucky Colonel of Kentucky Fried Chicken made that decision in his mid sixties. He was already on Social Security. He decided that he would become a winner with what he had in his hands…a receipt for delicious, golden fried chicken. The world has never been the same since.

The difference between a loser and a winner is "a will to win" and "a determination to win" regardless of how long it takes. Victory and defeat are sometimes only seconds or minutes apart. The turtle continued in the race. He was not as fast as the rabbit. He was not as talented as the rabbit. He was not a smooth talker like the rabbit. No one really expected him to win against the speedy rabbit, but he did. He persevered. He continued against all odds. He had a winner's attitude and…a big heart. He kept on going and won.

As I reminisce over the years of my life, the factor that I believe hinders us the most in our success as winners (mentally, physically, materially, spiritually) is the one word "guilt".

Sometimes, we condemn ourselves for the least little thing. Consequently and eventually, we build up a lot of guilt feelings…which eventually turn inward as anger. "Hurt feeling" are also anger in disguise. The burden of guilt and anger has no "place" in our lives. Yes, sometimes…the initial feeling of guilt or anger is warranted and merited. However, we do not have to continue to carry it around with us. When we mess up (screw up), we need to apologize, be penitent (sorry), and ask for forgiveness…and then move on and forget about it. God does. To forgive or ask for forgiveness takes action and courage. Winners have both.

Someone recently said, "At least 65% of all mental patients could leave today if they knew they were forgiven!" Most of them cannot bring themselves to "forgive themselves" of their past. This is tragic. We cannot change our past, but we can change our future…And our future is going to be a lot better than our past.

If we continue to condemn ourselves for something in our past...when, in fact...we have long since changed, we are condemning a person who is no longer guilty or even exists. Forgiveness eradicates the error and wrongdoing. We become a different person. Sometimes, we say, "If only I could live my life over again, I would do better. I would NOT commit the same mistakes again". If I could have another chance...If...If...If. This type of "thinking" is admirable and noble; however, it's NOT going to happen. It sounds good... feels good to say...but we have been allocated a certain number of days on this Planet...and I assure you, there will be no "re-runs" in our lives as we know them now.

Therefore, we can and should forgive ourselves and if we have wronged someone, we can and should make that wrong "right" by asking for forgiveness...if possible. The questions we need to ask ourselves are these: "What did I learn through this episode? How has this helped me to become a winner and a better person?"

The problem with living with "guilt" is that guilt and un-forgiveness cause us to relive our past over and over again...criticizing and passing judgment upon ourselves continually for past mistakes. Thus, this inevitably causes us to be unhappy and perhaps discontented with ourselves. See yourself as God sees you...forgiven and made whole. We cannot change our past. We can learn from it. We live in the present. We will never be able to go back in time and redo our mistakes or wrongs that we have committed. That won't happen. However, we can live today and live it the best way we can and then expect great things to happen.

SOMEBODY LOVES YOU INCREDIBLY
By

Somebody loves you MORE than you will ever KNOW.
Somebody is always thinking of you wherever you go.
Somebody really and truly cares.
Somebody loves you beyond compare.
And is concerned about every aspect of your welfare.
Never doubt for a moment that you are in the Lord's
      prayers.

You are a rare TREASURE and a tremendous FIND.
Do not waste anymore time,
In getting to know Him during this lifetime.
So please believe me when I say,
"Somebody loves you incredibly today."
And that somebody is Jesus Christ ALWAYS!

chapter

FIVE

Winning Attitudes From the Heart and Soul

We must learn to forgive ourselves. Forgive yourself and move forward! HOW: By actually feeling regret (being sorry) and remorseful for something that we did or perhaps should have done (omission). Since we are human beings, this happens to all of us at one time or another. We believe in the Golden Rule, "Do unto others as we would like for others to do unto us." Do we always practice the Golden Rule? No! The other side of the coin can be simply stated like this, "In accordance with the law of cause and effect, everything we "think" or say or do...will come back to us in like form."

The Bible says, "And forgive us our sins...just as we forgive those who sin against us" (Mt.6:12). Hence, this could be called the law of reaping and sowing. It now becomes clear to us that we can change our own course of events and destiny by forgiving and accepting forgiveness from others who might have hurt us in the past. Today is a great day to show forgiveness, mercy, compassion, and kindness to others! Let's do it.

Sometimes, we may "think" that the world does not have a clue as to how we feel, think, or live. Sometimes, we may think that society does not care or understand us. We may think that the world is so unsympathetic. Sometimes, we may wonder if our dreams will ever materialize. This is when we must reflect and think about how we feel about ourselves. Our community and our world will normally replicate in kind...the way we feel or think about our own selves. If we see ourselves strong and confident, the people around us will catch that attitude and also view us that way...even if on the inside, we do not possess the maximum self-assurance. William James once said, "The greatest discovery of my life...is that a man can change the circumstances of his life by changing his thoughts and attitudes."

As a man thinks in his heart, so is he. EVERYTHING we do is the result of our "thoughts" and "words". If we continually think positive...positive things will normally happen to us.

Once there was a man named "Jack Lack". Mr. Lack would say the most negative things like: "Good things never seem to happen to me. I am so unlucky. I always seem to be a day late and a dollar short! I just can't win! I just wish for once, I could get ahead. Nothing good happens to me anymore."

Have you heard Jack or someone like Jack Lack? Yes, we have all heard similar phrases. What is wrong with this picture? For one thing, this type of negative rhetoric is "self-fulfilling" prophecy. If Jack changes his "thinking", he will also change his verbal expressions...and this will change his life.

The Bible says, "For out of the abundance of the heart the mouth speaks. For whatever is in your heart determines what you say" (Lk.6:45). This Scripture works. I cannot tell you exactly why it works...But it does! It has worked for me and thousands of others. Our subconscious minds are invaluable computers. They compute the data in which we give them from our conscious minds.

For example, I cannot tell you how the air conditioning on a jet airliner works, but I can tell you this, it works...and I enjoy the comforts of it while in the air traveling at 500 to 600 MPH. Do I have to know the dynamics and theory behind the laws of air conditioning in order to enjoy the cool quality of air? No! But I do respect it.

As we change our attitudes, our "thinking" changes. As our "thinking" changes, we change. In accordance with the Law of Attraction, whatever we give...send forth...or convey to others, comes back to us in "like form". In Australia, they call this the "boomerang effect". This societal and natural law is NOT necessarily a command. However, if we ignore it, we will miss out on the greatest asset of all...Helping others as we help ourselves!

The Bible says, "A good person produces good deeds from a good heart" (Lk.6:45).

If I disrespect the Law of Gravity, I will get into deep trouble fast. If I respect the Law of Gravity, my life will be much easier. For example, a few years ago, I lived on the fourth floor of an apartment complex near Washington DC. Occasionally, I would go out on the balcony, enjoy a delicious cup of hot coffee, and experience the fresh air and calmness. However, if I had ignored the Law of Gravity, and jumped over the guard rail, my life would have ended with a sudden jolt when I landed. It would have been a fast ride though the air with inevitable results. Therefore, I will continue to respect natural laws.

Earlier, we talked about Mr. Jack Lack. He also seems to have another trait that alienates him from others. Jack is a constant complainer and whiner. He complains that life has little to offer him, yet he never "gives" anything back to society or to his community. The other day, Jack said, "Life just doesn't seem to have any meaning to me anymore!" What a sad commentary. Mr. Lack has never learned to respect the Law of Giving. What we give, we receive. If I sow happiness into others, I will reap/receive happiness myself. What I "put into" life or society, I will get back in like manner. We must never be afraid to give...For you see, whatever we give will always be replaced with much more...more than enough.

As we change our attitudes, we change. Our thinking changes. Our words change. Our lives change. Our whole outlook on life changes! Our words are powerful vehicles. They can create or destroy. Words are more powerful than nuclear bombs. You have heard that "sticks and stones may break my bones, but words will never hurt me". This is NOT true. Angry words have started wars. Loose words from loose lips have sunk ships. Defiant words have been the cause of thousands of deaths. We all know about Hitler and his angry words. Angry words have caused millions of divorces. Hospital research has found out that negative words during an operation...may contribute to the person's death. Words can become avenues to our hearts, souls, and spirits.

Be ready for change. Be ready for new paradigms As children, we were told what to expect as we got older...and older...and older. We were told to enjoy our youth because there would come a time when we would have to SLOW down to a snail's pace.

We watched our grandparents or other relatives say things like, "My legs hurt. My arms ache. I just don't seem to have any energy anymore. I hate old age. I wish I was 20 years younger. I feel like I'm dying." And the beat goes on...

In past generations, people literally talked themselves (with negative thinking) into physical deterioration, old age, and death. Why? Because they had been programmed during their whole lifetime to "believe" certain things about getting older. Life or age gives back to us what we "expect". It is really a horrendous tragedy to observe people whose false beliefs about "aging" have prevented them from enjoying the quality of life that they so richly deserve. I must re-emphasize: Our MIND controls every function of our body. The SUBCONSCIOUS accepts whatever suggestions are given to it...good, bad, or indifferent. The suggestions do not have to be valid or scientific. Our belief makes them true or not true. What we believe today will determine our future.

The Bible says, "Above all else, guard your heart, for it affects everything you do".

If I accept in my conscious mind that I will automatically slow down at 65 or 75 or 85...or whatever, my subconscious mind will accept that data...and make it so. We have what we say and think. My body will conform to my beliefs. That is why it is so important for me to say positive things about myself in reference to old age...or getting older. I must

NOT talk disease or infirmity. I need to talk strength, vitality, enthusiasm, and gusto. Our body wants to do what we tell it to do. Sometimes, our bodies and minds need encouragement from our lips. Do you get my drift?

Words are important to our well-being and health. Words that we speak give power to our thoughts...which make an indelible impression upon our subconscious minds. When we speak about old age, we need to speak in a positive fashion. We do not have to accept words of weakness, disease, or death. We need to govern our minds and establish a new paradigm so that we can live out our lives in dignity and longevity.

Medical doctors and gerontologists normally agree that the mental and physical capabilities of older people are far "under-rated". Over the years, they have learned that "senility" is NOT the result of physical decline, but is the result of pure boredom and sometimes...a feeling of uselessness.

We so often hear about "stress" in various people at various ages. What about the stress upon the older set? Many have been taught the following:
- As you get older, you will suffer from a loss of status.
- Your body will deteriorate rapidly.
- You will become a burden to your children.
- Your spouse will not want to be with you.
- You will see many of your friends get sick and die.
- You will experience purposelessness...
- Then you die!

Something is wrong with this picture. If an older person believes the above fallacies and erroneous beliefs, he will lose all hope and will be proven correct in his thinking. Then he dies!

The sad thing about this sort of thing is…It is completely unnecessary. It can be prevented. As we overcome false beliefs about aging and the aging process, we will live longer…be fully active longer…be healthy longer…and live a good wholesome and quality life until our longevity expires. Now, don't get me wrong. We will all die, but we do not have to die prematurely before our time. And we can all die with dignity and a sense of purpose and worth.

Think about this: Historically, significant creative inventions (64%) have come from people over 40. George Bernard Shaw won the Nobel Peace Prize at 69. Adenauer became chancellor of Germany at 73 and continued in that position until age 87. President Ronald Reagan was our President well into his 70s. Winston Churchill did not become Prime Minister of Britain until he was in his 60s. The Kentucky Colonel (Sanders) of Kentucky of Fried Chicken was over 62 years young when he came on the global scene with his secret chicken recipe. And do I need to say anything about the Senator from South Carolina…Senator Strum Thurmond who died at age 100?

I believe that we can be as happy as we choose to be! Happiness is a choice. It is a decision. I also believe that we can be active and truly alive for many years to come. Of course, this will depend upon our positive "thinking" and our positive "attitude".

Each human being has character. Each has dignity. Each has a purpose. Each has a destiny. Some individuals have great character and others not so great…some in high places…some not. Our character, nature, moral fiber, and personality are formed by the "way we think". Most often, our thinking habits are influenced by our associates, friends, parents, and mentors. As we grow older (mature), we start thinking more independently for ourselves. As free citizens, we no longer allow others to "think for us".

As our personality develops through the maturation process, we become aware of potential power that has perhaps...been lying dormant in our minds. We begin to realize that we can achieve certain things...we can succeed in life...we can have a "good wholesome life".

With a positive attitude, belief in ourselves, a good value system, and a thirst for knowledge, we can achieve "desired" results. In my past, there have been times that I let the intellectual and reasoning part of my mind (conscious) "talk me out of" success. After all, I had always been taught to "reason" things through...to rationalize...to verbosely explain things away.

Sometimes, we cannot always explain the way we feel or think, especially in our subconscious. In our hearts, it feels right. We just know it's the right thing to do...the right thing to say. Initially, we do not know how to explain it. It may NOT even be rational or "make good sense". But we have this vision, premonition, intuition, or hunch about something. We don't have the "words" for it yet, but we see it in our minds. Eventually, the vision, dream, or mental picture develops into a rough foundation...and later into a more structured idea and image...which eventually reaches fruition.

chapter

SIX

See Yourself as a Winner

WHO AM I? "My father died when I was five. I quit school when I was 16. By the time I was 17, I had lost 4 jobs already. I was married at 18...and a father at 19. When I was 20, my wife left me and took our baby daughter with her. Between the ages of 18 and 22, I had worked for the railroad...and failed...joined the Army and was booted out...failed at farming...applied for law school, but was rejected...Became an insurance salesman...and failed at that too. I couldn't do anything right. So, I became a cook and a dishwasher in a small café. I was grief stricken because I wanted my daughter back. I attempted to kidnap her, but even failed at committing this crime. Eventually, I talked my wife into coming back home. We both worked in the little café until I retired at 65. My 1st check from Social Security was $105.00. I felt rejected, defeated, demoralized, and discouraged. I decided to commit suicide. My life was not worth living. I went out behind our house and sat down to write my last will and testament. I began to write down what I had dreamed for my life. At that moment, I decided to take inventory of my talents. What could I do? I could cook. I was a great cook. I got up and went to the bank and borrowed $87.00... bought some boxes and chicken...fried the chicken...and went door to door selling my special recipe chicken. Who am I?" (Hint: KFC)

WHO AM I? My father was a wood chopper. I was a wood chopper. At the age of 21, I decided to read everything that I could find. I worked for awhile on a Mississippi ferry boat. I also worked in a general store, post office, on a farm, and even as a surveyor. I served in the state's militia. At 23, I ran for state congress and lost. However, at age 25, I was elected to the state congress. I passed the bar exam and became a lawyer at the age of 27. After going into practice for awhile, I went bankrupt. I fell in love with a beautiful young lady, but she died. I eventually married at age 33. We had four sons, but three of them died before reaching adulthood. At 35, I ran for office again...and lost. At 38, I was elected to Congress for one term. At 47, I ran for Vice President of the United States and lost. At 49, I ran for the US Senate...and lost. I was nominated for President at the age of 51...and won the election. Who am I?" (Hint: Honest Abe)

Why do some people win and others lose? Why are some successful and others are not? Some people expect to fail and they do. It's called anticipation of failure. We become what we think we will become. Be careful what you expect because you will probably get it. Some people always blame others. They will say things like: "It seems as if I get all the bad breaks. The reason I am not successful is…because the government has put too many regulations on me and my business. The bank won't give me the credit I need. This is why I cannot succeed."

Some will even blame their business and say, "My business failed." Businesses do not fail. People do. Some will blame their peers, boss, spouse, or even a physical handicap. Others walk in fear instead of faith. Fear is the most destructive force in the universe. It will sap the life and energy out of you. Fear cripples motivation. Fear will kill you. Fear destroys enthusiasm and creativity. Fear is a mental picture of what we do not want to happen. There are 350 Scriptures in the Bible that tell us NOT to fear. Job said, "The thing which I feared has come upon me. That which I was afraid of has happened" (Job 3:25). Job lost everything. Some say that it was because he feared the things that eventually came upon him.

As a winner with an incredible destiny, you will have some goals. Goals are very important. Know where you are going. Set some short term and long term goals. Your goals need to be written, specific, achievable, and believable. If you aim at nothing, you will hit your target…nothing. Goals bring purpose and order to our lives…if we pursue them. Anticipate success and it will come. See yourself as a winner. Think like a winner. Talk like a winner. Act like a winner. Develop some goals.

Winners embrace teamwork. We all have different personalities. This is the way God made us. This is what makes America the greatest nation on earth. Think about it. If every one was like you or me, this world would be a boring place to live. That's why we need each other. That's why we need teamwork. Personally, I have never met a man or woman in whom I couldn't learn something. We all have our varied gifts and talents. No one "person" ever knows more than the whole team or group. That's why we NEED Teamwork daily. We must learn how to continue to work together as a spirited and energetic Team. In teamwork, if we will promote each other, eventually, we will all get promoted. REMEMBER, "The man on the top of the mountain did not fall there. He climbed the mountain inch by inch and it became a cinch."

Over the years, I have found out a great secret. Never just sit back and take what life dishes out to you. MOST of the time, you must go after what you want. You must have a strong desire in your heart for it. Some people (even at the age of 65 or 70 or 80) are still waiting for their ship to come into the harbor...and for the captain of the ship to call their name and ask, "Where do you want your gold delivered?" This is not going to happen.

Remember Abraham Lincoln? He was a great man, orator, and President...not because he was born in a cabin, lived in a cabin, made a fire in a cabin, repaired the cabin, cooked in a cabin, and slept in a cabin. After a multitude of failures, he began to see himself as a winner. He developed some goals and got out of the cabin business. His goals made him a free man and a million others free as well. Goals have a habit of doing that...setting you free and those around you as well. Lincoln's dreams and goals made him a very prominent man in history...not the fact that he was born and reared in some farm cabin somewhere. That too, is history...But President Lincoln's success came when he decided NOT to just sit back and take what life had dished out to him and his fellow Americans. And the rest is history!

TEAMWORK
By Tommy Franks, Ph.D.

Communication is the key that unlocks the door.
Through challenging TEAMWORK, our programs will soar.
Our objectives, mission, and forum, we'll explore.
We must set the tone for many improvements and more.
We must work together as never before.
Professional Team Players are like gold ore.
The hotter the fire and the more you pour,
Each one seems to be refined and shouts, "Encore!"
Teamwork takes pride, action, and performance as esprit de corps.
Plans and programs are inevitable, we cannot ignore.
Furthermore, with teamwork and professional respect, we'll make a big score.
Communication provides tremendous results for Team Camaraderie and more.
You may be a janitor or a doctor or an executive in a large company store,
But you are still a team player and a tremendous depositor we cannot ignore.
Yes, you have pride, action, performance, and esprit de corps.
But with TEAMWORK and mutual respect, you'll continue to build and restore.
Remember, "Not one of us is as good as all of us." Forevermore!

Teamwork is not a one time deal. Success is failure turned inside out. Team players do not want to win once in a while. They want to win all the time. Winning becomes a habit in teamwork. Teamwork is the ability to work together toward a common vision, common goal, and the ability to direct individual accomplishments toward organizational objectives. It is the fuel that allows common people to attain uncommon results. "Coming together is a beginning; keeping together is progress. Working together is success" (Henry Ford).

To see yourself as a winner, you must find out what you want in life. The number one priority in life should be to determine what you want and what you want to do with your life. This may sound simple, but millions of people in the free world do not KNOW what they truly want. Some go through life not knowing what they really want out of life…and they get very upset with others when things do not turn out favorable for them. Know what you want and go for it with gusto.

I have asked people the question, "What do you want?" And they respond with, "Well, I do not know exactly. I think I may want this, but I am not sure. Sometimes I think I know what I want, but then I change my mind. I don't know what I want."

Some even give a spooky spiritual answer, like…"Well, whatever God wants for me is what I want. I just want to be in His will." This sounds nice, but it is a cop out. My answer to a person like this is: "Find out what God wants you to have and then pursue it. What does God want for you? What is His will for you?"

The person will normally respond, "Well, I don't know. I haven't asked Him yet. After all, I'm only 55 years old. How should I know?" What a cop out!

To see yourself as a winner, you will need to build a strong self-Image. How do you see yourself? Are you a winner? Your self-image is your source of personal happiness. It establishes the boundaries of your accomplishments. It more or less defines your limits. The following steps will assist you in improving your self-image:

1. See yourself as a winner. You must believe that you have a right to be successful. You were born to win, but may have been conditioned (by your environment) to lose. Your self-image will affect your performance.

2. Develop a positive attitude. Forgive yourself. Love yourself as God loves you.

3. Know who you are...and what you want out of life. Your self-image has nothing to do with "potential". Everyone has potential. But it has everything to do with your performance. Your self-image has nothing to do with what other people think of you, but everything to do with what you think of yourself. Think winner! Think about your destiny.

4. Eliminate self-pity. Some people go around feeling sorry for themselves all the time. They will tell you all their problems...all their troubles. Forget the past. It's gone forever. Think now. Think about where you are and where you want to be.

5. Associate with winners and positive people. Negative people will sap the very life out of you...which will eventually kill you. I heard a 94-year-old man say recently, "If you want to live long and be strong, stay away from old people." Why do you suppose he said that? Do think it might be that older people are sometimes negative and bent on dying? I call it the dying complex. Some people will tell you about every ache and pain they have had for the past 20 years. They sound as if they are already dead. Hello!

6. Read good books...inspirational and motivational. You will be the same person five years from now...that you are right now...except for two things...The books you read and the people you meet. Say positive things to yourself and about yourself (self-talk, affirmations). Develop goals.

chapter

SEVEN

Winning in the Workplace

WINNING in the workplace SHOULD be FUN. A few years ago when I worked in Washington DC, I wrote the following:

- "People who work for me normally love to come to work each day. "Why", you may ask? It is pretty simple. We treat one another with "respect, dignity, importance, and as professional adults". We treat each other the way that we would like to be treated. Our work environment is warm, friendly, family oriented, and professional. We treat all people as customers and with tremendous respect. We empower each other. Consequently, this wonderful environment produces very little stress and difficulties. We make working and learning fun.

- Our workplace has not always been so cordial and friendly. Our oasis did not happen overnight. Everyone of us has had to work at it. We now feel very good about ourselves because we have made it a supportive work environment.

- Winning means that we do not leave anything to chance. We have worked together to build a professional structure which includes "motivational management through participation (empowerment)". We have implemented our corporate values.

- As winners, we are proactive. We do not wait for our supervisors to initiate discussions about our job performance and job expectations. We check in regularly with our Senior Leaders and supervisors… and more importantly, with our fellow team players. They will tell us how we are doing. They will give us positive or constructive feedback…never negative feedback. Someone once said, "I like to give constructive criticism." Constructive criticism is still "criticism". Another word for criticism is faultfinding."

In today's society, our greatest challenge is learning how to work with others. We were NOT born with "people skills". They must be developed in all of us. This takes time and patience, especially to build teams with extraordinary accomplishments. This means teamwork, cooperation, and collaboration. This means leaving our big egos at the door. This means solving problems not only for the present, but also for the future. We must simultaneously develop solid professional relationships with others. Our greatest challenge in the "marketplace" is not the latest and greatest software or hardware package, but it is "working with people". As new employees continue to be acclimated into our workplace, we must learn NOT to judge individuals upon our first meeting. Remember: "Don't judge a book by its cover." We might be surprised at what we find inside. Accept people as you find them...NOT what you have heard about them. Give each person the benefit of the doubt. Allow their greatness to excel.

For the past 37 years, I have worked with some great individuals, teams, and organizations. I have found that the "truly great ones" knew how to work with people exceptionally well. However, some did not. Some worked with certain people well. Some did OK in certain situations. Nonetheless, almost inclusively, they all shared a common goal. They wanted to be more effective. They wanted good results. They desired to work well with others.

Today, to be truly successful as the "winners" we are, we must work effectively with others, regardless of our abilities. We must develop effective interpersonal relationships. This is what truly makes winners unique and separates them from non-winners. None of us is as smart or productive as all of us. We each have different strengths and talents. This is the beauty of working together. Positive Team Work will always have a positive impact on our performance, especially during a period of change. We all must adjust to change. Change is a part of every life on Planet Earth. Change always comes.

The better we get along with our co-workers, the easier our jobs will be. We will all win and perform better. It is always easier to work with people in whom we get along. Sometimes, this means putting aside our personal differences, idiosyncrasies, and peculiarities for the sake of the whole (the Team). Our attitude should be: "I win only if you win. We all win together." On the other hand, there may be a few people in our lives that "we just don't like" or per-haps they do not like us. We do not necessarily have to like them; however, we do have to be professional...and treat one another with dignity, respect, and professional cour-tesy. Working Together, We Can Make It Happen!

Finding wisdom in others is important. We should pair up with someone who has the skills and insight that we need...that will complement us. This is NOT necessarily a perfect person, but someone who can help us learn and get ahead. Some may call this person a "mentor".

Winning in the workplace is NOT eating and breath-ing our jobs. This is a sure-fire path to failure. If we live and breathe our jobs all the time, we will burn out quickly. We must maintain a healthy balance between our professional work and personal lives. We need to have fun, socialize, work, play, and have a well balanced and good quality life. Sometimes, after-hours activities for us and our coworkers give us a chance to interact on a non-working level which can actually strengthen our working relationships. This is where a good social committee gets involved; i.e., jazz con-certs, plays, dinners, picnics, or special sports events.

Damage Control is important at all times. Most employ-ees have failed at some point in their careers. I know I have. Do not panic when you fail. Don't get bent out of shape. Be honest. If you were at fault, share the blame and take a few notes...lessons learned. We are human beings, not machines.

If we love what we do, we will do it well. If we have pas-sion and enthusiasm about something, we will take the time to do it right.

As leaders, what's the thing we do more than anything else? Make decisions! Big ones, little ones, urgent ones, and not so urgent...Each requires much thought and time. This is when we need to delegate where possible. Some supervisors still say, "I'm in charge here. That means I'm supposed to make all the decisions." We know this is simply NOT true. However, it does mean that we are supposed to be sure that someone makes the decisions and that they are reasonable ones.

The mark of a good leader is not only hiring good people, but also training terrific people to make some of the important decisions...big or small. This is good for the supervisor and teams because it frees up his time to do even greater things. This is also good for the employee because it gives her control over some of the decisions and teaches each one more responsibility, develops greater trust, and enhances the overall morale.

In the workplace, it is simply not enough to make forward progress. For example, the football carrier was running ever so fast...with the crowd screaming to the top of their lungs. They were shouting. They were slinging their arms. They were jumping. They were giving some dramatic hand signals. The ball carrier could not make out what they were saying until he crossed the goal line. Then he heard, "Stupid, you were running in the wrong direction. You crossed the wrong goal line." When making progress, make sure it is not only forward, but also in the right direction. Stay focused while following your dream.

On your way to work, ask yourself the question, "What would I do today if I knew that it was impossible for me to fail? If I knew that it was impossible for me to make a bad decision?" Keep your eyes on your goals. Keep focused. Never say, "It's impossible."

Remember, you can be your own best friend or your own worst enemy. Say positive things to yourself; i.e., "Yes,

Handsome (or Beautiful), you are going to make it today. You will succeed. You are the apple of God's eye. Defeat is not a word in your vocabulary. Today is a brand new day of golden opportunities...just waiting to be fulfilled in your life."

chapter

EIGHT

Follow Your Dream with Passion

Winners follow their dreams with passion. They catch the "falling star". They look for the rainbow. They expect good things to happen and they do. They expect to win in the game of life. They expect success. Their dreams do come true. Have you ever of heard of Wally Amos? Mr. Amos founded "Famous Amos Cookies" several years ago... but not without trials of the greatest magnitude. He had a dream. He had passion to make it happen. He wanted to bake cookies. That's right...cookies. People said that his idea about cookies was crazy. Thank God, he didn't listen to them. He followed his dream and became very wealthy baking and selling cookies.

Wally believed in his dream and always said, "Solutions will come. Sometimes you have to reinforce your commitment. Get excited...Believe in yourself." The following is a POEM by Edgar Allen Guest that Wally Amos likes to quote:

"It Couldn't Be Done"

Somebody said that it couldn't be done
But he with a chuckle replied,
That maybe it couldn't, but he would be one who
    wouldn't say so
Until he had tried. So he buckled right in with a trace of
    a grin
On his face. If he worried, he hid it.
He started to sing as he tackled
The thing that couldn't be done and he DID IT.
Somebody scoffed, "Nay, you'll never do that.
Nobody has ever done it before."
But he took off his coat and hat and the first thing
That we knew, he had begun it.
With a lift of his chin and a bit of a grin...
Without any doubting or quitting, he started to sing
As he tackled the thing
That couldn't be done...AND HE DID IT !
Thousands will tell you that it can't be done.
Thousands will point out to you one by one all the dan-
    gers
That wait to assail you, BUT just buckle right in
With a bit of a grin. Just take off your coat and go to it.
You'll start to sing as you tackle the thing
That can't be done AND you'll do it.

Wally believed in his dream. He talked about his dream. He accomplished his dream. In today's world, we need to seek out people who have had a dream and then succeeded in accomplishing that dream. Learn what others are doing about their dreams. And then implement your own dream. No, it will not be easy, but dare to believe in yourself and you will do it. People with no dreams are like ships without rudders. You must have a game plan. You must clearly define your dream and know your purpose. Write out your dream. Rehearse it. Every successful man or woman has a dream.

Once you have the dream fixed firmly in your mind and heart, the subconscious mind goes to work immediately to bring these things into reality. The problem today is...less than 5% of the people put legs to their dreams. WINNERS follow their dreams with passion. We as human beings are built to have dreams. Dreams give us goals. Goals direct us straight to the target. Dreams give us PURPOSE. With passion, dreams give us direction, focus, and channeled energy. As winners, we must think, talk about, visualize, and write down our dreams. We have a destiny and passion to fulfill.

In a negative environment, sometimes it may not be in your best interest to SHARE your dreams with losers. Losers will try to dissuade you from carrying out your dream. Losers are not interested in your dreams. They are not interested in what is best for you. They will sap the energy and passion right out of you with their negative opinions. They often wear little T-Shirts that say, "It's all about me...No one else matters." They are concerned about what is best for them. Losers are selfish individuals. Furthermore, most people are not interested in what you want to do unless it affects them in some way. Therefore, use a lot of discretion and prudence in discussing your personal dreams with others. If you do share your dreams, try to share them with other dreamers and people with passion who have purpose, goals, and personal aspirations to be successful and change the world. One man or one woman can change the world. You can change the world.

Remember, dreams of passion and purpose come from God. He plants the dream seed in your heart. He made you for dreams. He created you to carry out your dreams. You are the BEST PRODUCT that He has ever produced. YOU are SPECIAL to God and to others. As you follow your dream with passion, you will develop qualities of confidence, determination, character, goodness, and self-esteem. God's blessings will assist you as you continue to act on your dream. Your perseverance and persistence will prevail. You are a very SPECIAL person.

Will adversity come? Yes, but because you believe in your dream...faith, hope, and love will put you over. You will use adversity as stepping stones. At times in my own life, I have vacillated, oscillated, wavered, equivocated, hesitated, and faltered. Other times, I have been indecisive, evasive, wobbly, swaying back and forth like a pendulum, even shilly-shallying; however, that only proves my point... Even though I am strong at times, I'm still a member of the human race. That's why I so desperately need to lean on the Creator of the universe at all times so that I can be successful in obtaining my dreams. If I were perfect, I would be in heaven. All of us are still under construction. Our passion must not waver in following our dreams.

In following our Dream with Passion, we must develop a Positive Attitude. The remainder of this chapter will be about attitude. It's that important!

The longer I live, the more I realize the importance of having a Positive Attitude. Attitude is more significant than so called facts. Attitude is more meaningful than the past, educational level, money, resources, circumstances, failures, successes, what we think, or what other people think...say...or do. A positive ATTITUDE is golden...and will make you rich as you fulfill your dream and destiny.

Great results have been achieved through dreams. We are productive citizens that are indebted with an attitude of gratitude to God in achieving our goals, objectives, purpose, dreams, and destiny. Remember this: "For God is not unrighteous to forget your work and labor of love, which you have shown toward His Name, in that you have ministered to the saints, and (continue to) minister" (Heb:6:10).

Attitude is more substantial than mere appearances, giftedness, skills, or talents. Look at companies that have folded in the past few years. Attitude will make or break a company...corporation...home...or...church. It will also make or break you or me. The remarkable thing is we have a choice. We can "sit around" and be negative or we can embrace a good attitude and go forward. We do not have to be melancholy or despondent. We can change our attitude. No one else can do this for us. We are responsible. This thing is in our hands.

None of us can change the place, date, or circumstances in which we were born into this world. We had no control over who our parents were. We had no control over when we were born. We had no control over where we were born. We cannot change our past. People will act or respond in certain ways. We cannot change the inevitable. HOWEVER, we can change our attitudes to be receptive and responsive in a positive manner. Personally, I believe that life is 10% of what happens to us and 90% of how we respond to it. Who is in charge of your life? Who is in charge of your attitude? Is it you? Is it your spouse...your parents...

your children? You and I alone are in charge of our attitudes.

Someone once said, "A company may spread itself over the whole world, may employ thousands of men and women…have the best product in the world; yet, the average person will form an opinion of the company through the CONTACT of one INDIVIDUAL. If that person is rude or inefficient, it will require a lot of courtesy and efficiency to overcome the bad impression. EVERY member of an organization is a salesperson. The first impression that is made is an advertisement…good or bad."

So as you can see, ATTITUDE is so very important in activating our dream…which is significant to all of us, especially as we interact, mingle, and socialize with others. The problem many times is that we are surrounded with naysayers… those who say that we cannot succeed, those who ridicule us, those who are perhaps jealous of us, and those who say that we cannot make it. When this is the case, we need to cut ourselves loose from negative voices and losers. Put one winner into a group of nine losers and before long, the winner will begin to talk and act like the other losers. Thus, she loses her dream that was once so vivid, vibrant, and vital.

Someone once said that a pessimist is a person who… regardless of the present…is disappointed in the future. A wise person (John Wooden) said, "Do not let what you cannot do interfere with what YOU can DO."

"It is a FACT that you and you only project who you are to others" (Norman V. Peale).

Many times, I have said a lot about looking in the mirror every morning and talking to yourself. WHY? Because we behave in a manner that is consistent with the way we see ourselves. If you view yourself as a successful individual, your actions will follow through with every effort to make that happen. Eventually, you will see your goals and dreams fulfilled. We make our own destiny. We dream our own dreams. We do. No one can cause us to fail...but us. I cannot blame anyone else for my failures, problems, shortcomings, idiosyncrasies, or peculiarities...BUT ME. I must take the responsibility for my own life.

In accomplishing our dreams with passion, a good attitude is not only "getting a life", but it is also "being responsible for your life and actions". "Do not let what you cannot do interfere with what you can do" (John Wooden). Take a good look at yourself. What do you see? What do you really see? Do you see a positive individual or negative individual? We BEHAVE in the manner and way in which we see ourselves. Someone once said that quitting is a permanent solution to a temporary problem.

William James said, "The greatest discovery of our generation is that human beings can alter their lives by altering their minds." This morning I got out of bed on the right side. Sometimes, I get out of bed on the left side. Does it really matter on which side I get up? I personally believe that it is all "in the mind" and attitude.

"The greatest MISTAKE a person can make is doing nothing" (John Maxwell).

If you believe you can do something, the chances are... you can. If you BELIEVE that it is impossible, the chances are...you are right. However, if it looks impossible, but you somehow BELIEVE that you can do it anyway, the chances are...you will. An old King Solomon proverb says, "As a man thinks in his heart, so is he."

Is life fair? No. Is our justice system fair? No! Do we have inequities in this life on Planet Earth? Yes! How do we react to inequities? Do we sometimes have difficulties with other people? Then pinch yourself because you are very much alive and living a normal life. We are measured by the winds of adversity, the heat of the fire/furnace, the grinding of metal (iron sharpens iron), and the elasticity of our strengths. No one has ever trained to fight a war by sitting around the camp fire on a warm summer night eating bun buns, roasted hot dogs, and homemade ice-cream. A good soldier is a soldier seasoned by adversity.

As we all know, our attitude determines our altitude. Attitude: Its roots are inward. Its fruit is outward. It either draws or repels others. It can be our friend or our enemy. Vince Lombardi said, "It is not whether you get knocked down; it is whether you get up." Albert Einstein said, "In the middle of difficulty lies an opportunity."

Attitude is: A state of mind or a feeling…disposition, the way a person carries himself…the way one views things… positive or negative.

Volition is: The exercise of the will, voluntary action… conduct. Attitude can be displayed or affected by one or more of the following:
- Conduct, behavior, demeanor, or posture
- Tone of voice, gesture, style, manner, presence
- Thinking, mood, feeling, morals, principles, ideals, lifestyle

"Being a sex symbol has to do with an attitude…not looks. Most men think that it is looks. Most women know otherwise," said Kathleen Turner in 1986.

"Our attitude toward our own culture has recently been characterized by two qualities, braggadocio (bragging all the time) and petulance (having a bad temper). Braggadocio is empty boasting of American power, American virtue, and American know-how which has dominated our foreign relations for decades. Here at home within the family, so to speak, our attitude to our culture expresses a superficially different spirit, the spirit of petulance, bad temper, and irritability. Never before, perhaps, has a culture been so fragmented into groups, each full of its own virtue, each annoyed and irritated at the others" (Daniel J. Boorstin 1960).

"Art is the child of Nature; yes, her darling child, in whom we trace the features of the mother's face, her aspect and her attitude" (Henry W. Longfellow 1807-82).

Dale Carnegie said, "The successful man (woman) will profit from his mistakes and try again in a different way." Another great person said, "What lies behind us and what lies before us are tiny matters compared to what lies within us" (Walt Emerson).

Try this sometime: Look in the mirror and say, "I may not be able to change the whole world around me, but I can CHANGE the WAY I see the world WITHIN me. I can do that. I will do that."

Furthermore, talk to yourself some more and say, "You are the BEST thing...since jelly beans. No one is like you. You are unique and SPECIAL in every way. Out of 6.3 billion people, you are the only you. Today, you can influence and affect those around you."

A winner with a good attitude is a person who affects change and things. You can affect change, people, and things...today. You can affect others in a positive way. You can posture yourself with a sense of humor, passion, and active productivity. You can smile. You can have a warm attitude. You can follow your dream. The choice is yours.

Are you still with me? Do you still have a mirror? Good, let's talk to ourselves some more. "Self, I have been watching you lately. You need to rest a little. You need to take yourself less seriously. You need to relax a little more. Smell the coffee. Smell the roses. Take some time just for you. Be calm. You are a tremendous person of worth. You have genuine affections, great qualities, intelligent instincts, great passion for living, and feelings of gifted talents and abilities. You are a dreamer with passion."

As I said earlier, you can do it. You have character. You have inherited characteristics of strength. This is the way you were made. Today, this moment, you are free from any inferiority, self-consciousness, weakness, and detrimental habits. You are a free moral agent to make good sensible and intelligent decisions that will profit you in your dream world. Today, you go forward with a greater sense of responsibility and accountability for your fellow man.

"When and if things go wrong, don't go with them" (Roger Babson). "You are today where your thoughts have brought you; you will be tomorrow where your thoughts take you" (James Allen).

"Winning is not everything...but making the effort to win is" (Vince Lombardi). "You never achieve real success unless you like what you are doing" (Dale Carnegie).

"You and I do not see things as they are. We only see things as we are" (Herb Cohen).

NOW FOR THE REAL KICKER: "Whether you think you can or think you can't...You are right" (Henry Ford).

In this day and time...with people ever so BUSY, we often want to correct the other person's attitude most of the time. We see "them" at fast food restaurants, grocery stores, the mall, church, auto dealerships, traffic jams, schools, home, and especially at our WORK environments. In my six decades of living on Planet Earth, I have found out a very high-level and important SECRET: The most expedient way for me to skillfully reduce the tension in the air is to CORRECT my own attitude. Is it easy? No...especially for a "Type-A" individual...It is not an easy chore, but it is absolutely neces- sary for my own welfare...both physically and progressively. In this life, there will always be individuals who we think are airheads, hotheads, deadheads, and utter nincompoops... But we must keep a good attitude if we are to be success- ful. We are still human whether we vocalize it or not. Hence, it is how we adjust, accommodate, and handle the situa- tion that really matters. We can change our own attitude or "go ahead" and get an ulcer if we want. It is our choice.

John Maxwell said, "God chooses what we go through; we choose how we go through it. Your attitude determines your actions. Your actions determine your accomplish- ments."

Someone has said, "We cannot direct the wind, but we can adjust our sails."

I have personally found out in life that once I say that I am beaten, I am. If I want to win in the game of life, I must have the right attitude and my actions must match that of my speech. If I say that I can't do a certain thing, then I can't. The converse of that is: If I say that I can do it, the battle is 95% won. As you may have found out, the victory does not always go to the strongest, most knowledgeable, or the most talented...You have found out in life that sooner or later, the man who gains the victory as a winner is the individual who THINKS he CAN. Attitude determines altitude...and altitude determines our dreams.

"A successful man is one who can lay a firm foundation with the bricks that others have thrown at him" (David Brinkley). And people will throw bricks at you...if you are doing anything. The only way that this is not true is...If you are doing nothing with your life...and even then...you will be criticized. Therefore, make life count for something...and don't worry about what others are saying. Believe in yourself. Dream big. Victory will come. Pick your right foot up and place it in front of you toward your goal and the victory is 75% won. Take the left foot and do the same thing and the victory is 95% won. Then continue to focus, take high aim, pull back the string on the bow, and let the arrow go...BULLS EYE. With a great attitude like that, no one can stop you...except you.

We have a choice everyday regarding our dreams and the attitude that we embrace. We cannot change our past. We cannot change other people! The only thing that we can change is ourselves and our attitude. Life is 90% how we react to it.

A genuine leader displays a positive attitude and projects this attitude to others. Positive people attract. People will not follow someone who is frustrated, always disappointed, and filled with negatives. There are many individuals that do a lot of things right; however, their negative attitude keeps them from succeeding.

The single most IMPORTANT ingredient to success is a Positive Attitude. Negative people drain our batteries. They tend to drag us down. We soon start avoiding them. People look for people who are positive. The whole world is looking for inspiration, enthusiasm, and a positive force. Positive people dream big...excite, motivate, and inspire others.

Attitude is a little thing that makes a BIG difference. Keep your face to the sunshine and you cannot see the shadows. If it is to be, then it is up to me. Attitude is the way we think. Our attitude is something that other people can see. They can see it in our voice...the way we move...our facial expressions...and feel it when they are with us.

Our attitude expresses itself in everything we do, all the time, wherever we are. Positive attitudes invite positive results. Anything we do with a positive attitude will work for us and not against us. A positive attitude is always looking for ways to solve problems. Attitude makes the difference in everything we do during our entire life. Positive attitudes can be developed by emphasizing the good and by refusing defeat.

Bottomline: In order to follow our dreams with passion, we must develop a Positive Attitude.

chapter

NINE

You Have a Winner's Destiny

We learn something from every single book or article that we read. I believe that every single person on Planet Earth is special and has dignity, a destiny, and great worth. He or she has intelligence. She is created by the Master Carpenter. She has the five senses, intellect, emotions, desires, ambitions, and initiative. Man/Woman is spirit. The real person is spirit. This is the only way man can communicate with God...our Creator. Even though man lives in a body, he communicates with his soul and spirit. Therefore, I want to challenge you to look within and begin to communicate with the God of the universe because our final destiny is Heaven. A Winner's Destiny is Heaven!

"...The Kingdom of Heaven is like unto a merchant man, seeking goodly pearls...Who, when he had found one pearl of great price, went and sold all that he had, and bought it" (Mt.13). You are that "pearl of great price". One human being is worth more than the entire world or a thousand worlds. You are worth more than all the gold and silver and diamonds in the entire universe. You are God's child and you are destined for the throne.

You were **Born to Win**. Life and abundance is a choice. In brief, it is God's will that you prosper, be in good health, and have healthy emotions in your every day life activities. It is His will that you be free from any dependency that would cause you to miss out on any of His magnificent blessings. It is God's will that you be free indeed and "in charge" of your own faculties. As a winner, you will commit to quality living, freedom living, and financial freedom. You have dignity and you have a wonderful destiny.

Show me your friends and I will show you your future. Show me whom you run around with and I will show you what you can expect. Follow the road or trail to your dreams...not the path that others expect you to take. God has blessed you with the freedom to SOAR. You must have the courage and faith to believe...and have the will to succeed. Someone said, "Worry is the crabgrass of the soul." Someone else said, "He is not a failure. He is not dead yet."

"For by your words you will be justified, and by your words you will be condemned" (Mt.12:37). Words either bring a blessing or a curse. An idle or negative word may fall into the soil of someone's heart and poison his life forever. Think about it. You are judged by your tongue and speech. Let your tongue become the pen of a ready writer.

God made you special. You are the "only you". He formed your inward parts while you were still in your mother's womb. You are fearfully and wonderfully made. God fashioned you, designed you, appointed you, and brought you into this world. You are marvelously and incredibly made. You are the ONLY you that will ever be made or created. You are made of water, fluid, calcium, iron, carbon, lime, fiber, and other tissue. You have 263 bones, 970 miles of blood vessels…20,000 hairs in your ears alone. You have 10 million nerves and nerve endings, 600 million air cells in your lungs. Your heart beats 4200 times an hour and pumps 24,000 pounds of blood every 24 Hours.

Even when you were only an embryo, you were in the mind of God. You are the "apple" of His eye. You are the BEST product that heaven has ever produced. According to the Bible, God has even written a book about you which contains all the days of your life. God planned each of your days before you were born. You are special. You are destined for the throne room.

You were NOT born by accident no matter what. Regardless, whether your parents were married or not married…you were NOT born illegitimately in His eyes. You were born on PURPOSE. God has a plan for your life. Your mother or father cannot give life. Only God can give life to form a human being and create a baby. God never does anything by accident or carelessly. Everything He does, He plans on purpose…not happenstance. You were created by God on purpose with a plan and with an eternal destiny. God saw you before the existence of the foundation of the world. You were not born by accident. There are no accidents with God. You are here by Divine appointment, providence, and destiny.

Now, what does all this mean? You were Born to Win. You must dare to BELIEVE in YOURSELF and value yourself.

God does. God has confidence in YOU. This may be difficult for some to accept, but it is true. Your POTENTIAL is determined by God, not circumstances or other people. When God created vegetation, He spoke to the earth (dirt) and it was so. When God made the stars, He spoke to the sky (firmament or second heaven) and it was so. When God wanted fish, He spoke to the waters. When He created animals, He spoke to the earth (land, dirt, and soil). But when He created Man (You), He spoke to Himself. He said, "Let Us make man in Our Image."

You are created to be like God...not God, but to be like Him (spirit, soul, and body). You need to use your God given talents, abilities, and the POTENTIAL that God has instilled within you. Dare to believe in yourself. The more you value yourself, the greater your self-esteem will become. Individuals with great self-esteem will do great things. Greatness can never be achieved unless we value ourselves and feel good about ourselves. As you value yourself, you will find out that you really do have control over your life. Some people believe that "life" is something that just happens to you...that you are powerless to do anything about it. This is NOT true. Life is what we make it. We make choices. We make decisions. We have a will. We are free moral agents. God is aware of everything about you. He created you to be a powerful person through His only Son...Jesus Christ.

One thing that will assist us in developing good self-esteem is: A good work ethic. Working a plan that will assist us in our livelihood builds self-esteem. We need to work our plan and NOT make excuses when things go wrong. If you are still breathing, things will go wrong occasionally. Working and achieving something good with our skills and abilities will directly link our performance to self-esteem. We do have control over our lives.

In order to have a Winner's Destiny, we need to change. We must learn to change. Change is always possible regardless of an individual's age. It takes discipline to change. We do NOT like change normally, but change will come...whether we like it of not. To obtain the finer things in life, we must change. Some people fear change, yet we are changing every single moment. You are not the same person you were yesterday. Today, you are a "brand new" you. Feel good about yourself. Allow enthusiasm and joy to fill your life.

Share with someone today by saying something positive and edifying that will motivate them to higher ground. If they are happy, be happy with them. If they are excited, be excited with them. We are not only earthen vessels, but we are also filled with God's abilities and His Spirit. No, we are not perfect...just forgiven.

Look in the mirror and say, "You're a fine piece of work. You're a tremendous person to know. You get better with each passing day. Today, I will ENJOY life. My life is precious. I am a child of the Creator. I will make it and I will make it happen for others."

The story that you are about to read is a true story about two beggars (Lk.16). Let's call these beggars, Laz and Dives. Dives had all kinds of money. He was RICH...had money coming out of his ears. He wore the finest threads that money could buy. He drove the finest luxury cars and trucks. He continued to make more and more long, green backs everyday. Dives had gobs of money and all kinds of bank accounts. Dives had it made on Planet Earth. He had everything. He had it all. He dined and wined and partied every single day. He became a partying fool...

But along comes Laz (Lazarus)...a different kind of beggar...HUNGRY...SICK...COLD...HOMELESS. He made his bed at the gate of Dives' mansion. All he wanted was to be fed with the crumbs that fell from Dives' table. MOREOVER, the dogs came and licked his sores and old LAZ received no comfort at all. In a little while, LAZ died. The angels grabbed LAZ (the poor beggar) and carried him to Paradise (Abraham's Bosom).

A little later, DIVES (the partying fool) also dies. BUT old DIVES ends up in HELL.

Now DIVES (the rich beggar) realizes he has been involuntarily taken to his own Bar-B-Q...and before long he realizes that he is about to be cooked. He is in torment...the flames of the fire begin to burn his backside. Furthermore, old DIVES is sensitive to heat, especially to an open FLAME. His hide does not take too kindly to this red hot fire.

Suddenly, old Dives begins to beg. He begs for water. He becomes one of many beggars in hell. Low and behold, he looks up and sees Father Abraham in Paradise...and guess who else? That's right...OLD LAZ, the beggar from Planet Earth. But the tides have now changed. Laz is now known as KING LAZ and has it made. Most of his days are spent eating caviar and sipping heavenly wine. He now wears the finest threads from SAX, 5th AV, Planet Heaven. He doesn't have a care about anything...could give a hoot less about anything. King Laz has it made in the heavenly shade...His final destiny.

Beggar DIVES (the one who use to be rich on earth) decides to run a game on Father Abraham. He said, "Father Abraham, have PITY and MERCY on me. My backside is on fire and I'm over cooked already. This flame is tormenting me and turning me to charcoal. Father Abraham, please, I beg of you...have somebody to check out the air conditioning in this place. It doesn't seem to be working! And if you would please, send King LAZ with a cool glass of water so that he can dip his finger in the water and COOL my tongue. My, my, but I'm thirsty."

Father Abraham speaks, "Beggar Dives, don't you remember on Planet Earth when you drove around in your Mercedes Benz and BMW and Alfa Romero...and old LAZ walked...crawled...and hopped everywhere he went? You ate steak...He ate dog food. You drank wine...He drank left over stale tea and three day old coffee. You wore fur, leather, and mink...He wore rags. BUT NOW, times have changed. Your life on Planet Earth has ended. You are in hell with fire and brimstone. King LAZ is in Paradise with me. You will now be Bar-B-Qed and fried to a crisp, but old LAZ will continue to wine and dine with me and the Messiah forever. NO, I cannot send LAZ to you. Besides, there is a big gulf or chasm between us. Those that would want to pass from here to you cannot. REALLY, man, who in his right mind would even want to go where you are...GET REAL, FOOL!"

DIVES continues to try to run a game on Old Father Abraham, but Abraham is too smart for him. Dives says, "Since I am now a beggar in hell, I beg of you, please send King Laz to my Daddy's home at 555 Blue Street, Ding Dong, USA. I've got five brothers there. I beg of you...Please. I don't want them to come here and be Bar-B-Qed like me."

Abraham replies, "The Scriptures, God's Holy Word, has warned them time and time again. Your brothers can read the Bible anytime they so desire. They can go to church. They can repent. They can be saved if only they would believe in Jesus Christ.

DIVES starts grabbing at straws. He says, "No, Father Abraham...YOU don't UNDERSTAND. One of my brothers is a dope pusher and pothead. Another one is a pimp and butthead. The third one is a crooked banker and pinhead. My fourth brother is a real estate swindler, lawyer, and infidel. My fifth brother (Shiftless Sam) has never earned an honest dollar in his whole life. Please, Mr. Abraham, you have got to help me. I am desperate. My brothers won't go to church...they won't read the Bible...they won't repent... BUT, if a GHOST were to visit them, they would REPENT and BELIEVE! Just send Old LAZ back there as a Ghost and then they will believe."

Abraham responds, "If they won't listen to God's people whom they have seen or believe the Word of God which they can see, touch, and read, they certainly won't believe some GHOST or disembodied spirit from the dead."

What is the moral here? Caring for others is one of the best ways in the world to be a winner in this life. Caring and valuing others is what winners do. I believe that if Dives (the rich man) would have cared and helped Lazarus (the beggar) while on earth, his destiny would have been much different. We get out of life what we put into it. "Do unto others as you would have them to do unto you."

You have an incredible destiny...Heaven. You were born to live on this earth for a number of years and then go to Planet Heaven. This is what God had in mind for you from the beginning...even from the foundation of the world. As you travel through life, you will be given golden opportunities to live out your identity and purpose. At the end of your journey, you will transition to a higher plane...Heaven.

Some people want to die and go on to heaven without really fulfilling their purpose or truly living life to its fullest while on earth. God has a Divine purpose and plan for you. He has given you your true identity. He has given you security, acceptance, and wisdom. God wants us to live life LARGE and not die prematurely.

Our past failures do not determine our identity or destiny. Current feelings do not determine our identity. Our jobs and positions do not determine our identity or destiny. However, our identity is somehow wrapped up in our destiny. Read on...

Our Identity Versus Our Destiny!
By Tommy Franks

Dark times come and they go,
Even pain sometimes overflows.
We do have an escape...
And the Christ Child is never too late.

What do we do during difficult times?
We remember who we are and continue to be kind.
Since we did not make ourselves, we remember Whose
       we are....
He is never too far!

We must stand for justice, illumination, and the light
Because the darkness has no might or insight.
Our Creator will repay us for the years that the locusts
       have eaten,
Even though at times, we may feel warn out and
       weather-beaten.

The One Who made us has determined our value
To be neither average, casual, or on Lost Avenue.
We can continue to have peace even during the
       storm,
Because the sun will shine again tomorrow morn.

We are loved beyond compare.
We can take the mountain...if we dare!
Our identity is not based on our performance or man,
But our destiny is based on our lives transformed and
       enhanced.

Our identity is not based on our past failures or circum-
    stance,
Nor is it based on our parents per chance.
Our jobs, skills, and talents do not identify
Who we are in this world so intensified.

Who then, determines our identity and destiny today?
Not only do we, but the Man of Galilee also persuades
    day by day.
He is bigger than any problem we face in these vessels
    of clay.
He is with us forever to stay.

chapter

TEN

Aim High

Aim High! My son is a pilot and knows what it is to aim high. Currently, he is aiming at the moon. Don't laugh. One thing for sure is...he will never shoot himself in the foot by aiming at the moon. Set positive goals and aim high.

To aim high, you must have goals. When you are making goals, do not worry about your feet. As long as your head and heart are going in the right direction, your feet will follow. Do not always tackle your aspirations and ambitions with huge goals. More importantly, start with realistic and obtainable goals...inch by inch. When making goals, get the big picture. Be reasonable, but do not think too small. Sometimes big goals create a fear of failure. Do not fear. Don't think in a mediocre fashion. The alternative is to make no goals at all...which guarantees failure. This is what the lazy man does...makes no goals. Start out small and slow...follow up with larger goals as you are successful in achieving the little goals.

Some people want "fast" goals. Mr. Jones will say things like, "I want this done speedily." Mr. Smith laughs and responds, "You want it when?" Goals and forward progress have nothing to do with speed, but everything to do with DIRECTION. Sometimes to attain a goal, you must stay focused for years. The important thing is...to continue to move toward your goal...whether it is a short or long range. Remember the experience between the rabbit and the turtle? The rabbit took his eyes off the goal. He waffled, loafed, malingered, wasted precious time, and eventually napped. He came in second place which was also last place. Sorry, but no cigars!

Goals should be placed under our control if they are our goals. We cannot control our destiny if the goals we have set are under someone else's control, command, or direction. We must be able to see the target and focus on the target...even if it is miles or years away. Once you have located the target in which the goal resides...Aim, focus, zero in, and pull the trigger. Even if you miss the first couple of times, continue to be decisive, tenacious, persistent, determined with purpose...And you will hit the target, thus reaching your goal.

Some individuals want all objections, concerns, problems, and difficulties solidified prior to making goals. These people will always be in a rut. A rut is nothing more than a casket with both ends kicked out. They will always make excuses why certain things happen (or don't happen) in their lives. They have no goals.

To be successful, we must have the right tools or as some may call it...the right stuff or right ammunition. Sometimes, this may mean additional education or training in which to achieve our goals. If an archer takes his bow out to the range and properly aims "dead center" at the target, but has no arrows, success of hitting the bull's eye is about nil. We need to aim high and we need to have the best possible ammunition (tools) in which to reach our target (goal).

To aim high, we also need to develop some good habits. This is a fact of life. Our habits need to lead us toward success. They need to contribute to our financial welfare. They need to help us win at the game of life. To develop good habits is not an easy task. Previous bad habits are hard to die.

We must become organized. We must see the purpose of our lives. When we begin to organize our minutes, hours, and days, we will begin to focus and achieve what is best for us. Our energy will be channeled in the right direction. We will begin to accomplish our dreams and develop good habits and goals.

We must NOT put things off. Every day is a new day, but we must have a specific plan for each day. In addition to goals, we must have structure. We need to develop good habits. According to psychologists, it takes 21 days to form a habit...good or bad. Good habits bring success. Bad habits bring just the opposite of success...failure. Bad habits are hard to break. We must admit that we are powerless without good habits to assist us in our achievements. Our lives can become manageable through discipline, structure, good habits, and having a purpose for each day.

You were **Born to Win**. By now you have learned that you cannot do it all by yourself. You have come to realize and believe that the Creator is the only Person Who can truly help you to develop good habits. Most of the time, our minds are on other things...not "developing better habits". Our minds and bodies do not want to cooperate.

We must aim high. Aiming high is commendable. The enigma is: If we aim too low and we hit it, what have we accomplished? We must Aim High.

God prepared Heaven for YOU from the foundation of the world. God knows you, your ways, your thoughts, your words, and every hair on your head. You are the very best product that the Father God ever produced. You mean more to Him than the whole world. There is nothing that He will NOT do for you...if it's profitable for you and benefits your life.

You can develop your full potential. Have you ever looked at the seed of a pine cone? Even though it is only a seed, it has the POTENTIAL to be a FOREST. What do you see when you look at this seed? Do you see a forest or only a simple tree? Everything in the whole wide world has POTEN-TIAL. You have unlimited potential.

What is "Potential"? It is dormant ability, reserved power, un-tapped strength or resources, unused SUCCESS. Potential never retires. Most people die without ever devel-oping their FULL potential. No wonder it has taken us so long to develop our natural resources.

Did you know that some of our forefathers have robbed us? That's right. Some of them have robbed us blind. They died with songs, books, inventions, discoveries, sermons, medical knowledge, and talents...and took them to their graves without giving them to us. They have robbed this generation of their latent ability. A man or woman has no right to die and go to his grave without developing those new discoveries or medical cures that were given to them long before they passed away.

Some of them had the potential for great service to humanity, but just simply decided not to do it. They died with incredible ideas, inventions, and medical cures locked up on the inside of them. How tragic it is when unused and unreleased ability and potential go to the grave without action and development.

What now? We live and learn from the mistakes of others. Failure is not the absence of success. FAILURE is the ABSENCE of TRYING. The person who says it can't be done is normally the person who is standing in the way of the person who is doing it.

I believe we can maximize our full potential. Why? Because we have "zeal" which means: Eager desire, earnest enthusiasm, passion, energy, drive, and fervor. I believe this generation will maximize their full potential. We have been created to win. We must dare to believe in ourselves… and aim high.

Most men and women only live a fraction of their full, creative potential. Each of us could probably be so much more alive, alert, loving, dynamic, and creative. We have the potential to be so much more. What is the key to full human potential? I believe it is knowing who you are in the Kingdom of God. He has created you in His image.

Deep within each of us lies a field of pure, unlimited, creative potential and productive resources. We were created for GREATNESS. We were created for SUCCESS.

Expect SUCCESS. Aim high. Success will come. YOU are SPECIAL to God and to others. You are special to your children. You are special to your friends and you should feel special to yourself. WHY? Because it is true. You have inside qualities of confidence, determination, character, goodness, and the anointing of God. As you use your potential, your perseverance and determination will be activated.

As you develop good habits, follow your dream, aim high, and become responsible for your own actions, you become a powerful and positive force in winning. What do we mean by being responsible? Being responsible is being accountable for our own actions. Every person is responsible for his own actions...no exceptions. I cannot blame my wife, mother, father, sister, brother, children, or dog for my behavior. I own my actions. I own my baggage. I own the decisions that I have made...no one else. I cannot blame others or make excuses for my life or the journey that I have traveled. I made the choices.

All of us have an obligation and responsibility to people. People are the product of heaven, not earth. The body is earthy, but not the real person. Being responsible not only helps you to be a better person, but it also helps others to achieve their dreams and personal goals as well. We have a responsibility to bring out the best in others. Being responsible means that we do not have to manipulate, coerce, intimidate, provoke, accuse, dominate, or castigate other people. When we care for others, we become responsible. We become less selfish. We become compassionate.

A responsible person will NOT embarrass others. She will go out of her way to ENCOURAGE people. The whole world is looking for responsible people because they are rare.

Expect the very BEST of others and eventually you will get their best. No, it's not easy, especially when most people have low expectations of themselves. Life gives us whatever we will accept. People treat us the way we allow them to treat us.

If we accept failure, we will have plenty of it. But if we expect SUCCESS, it will come. If we accept mediocrity, we will never be more than average. WHO wants to be average? Life is too short to be unhappy, poor, defeated, and uneventful. People will rise to the standards that we set for them. In following our dreams, we need to aim high, be responsible, broaden our horizons, and raise our standards, goals, and aspirations.

There is more to a person than what you see on the outside. You never KNOW what's wrapped up in a piece of hide. Therefore, we must be responsible and treat individuals with dignity and respect. The past is gone. Today is a brand NEW day filled with opportunities. Because you are responsible, you have inside qualities of confidence, determination, character, and good common sense. You realize that inside qualities are more important than outside appearances.

In order to aim high and reach our target, we must be responsible. A responsible person does NOT want something for nothing. He is not looking for a handout. He is looking for opportunities to give and serve others. None of us is born acting responsibly. We learn to act responsibly. A responsible character is formed over time. It is made up of our thoughts, actions, and daily habits associated with our feelings. Responsible people try to do what is right. They have the courage and self-control to act decently, even when tempted to do otherwise.

We want our children to appreciate the importance of being responsible. We also want them to develop the habits and strength to act responsibly within society. Learning to be responsible includes learning to respect and show compassion for others. It means being honest. It means to show courage in standing up for our principles. Being responsible is learning to develop self-control in acting on our principles. It is also maintaining self-respect for ourselves and respect for others. As part of being responsible, we need to respect and show concern for the well-being of other people. Respect ranges from using basic manners to having compassion for the suffering of others. Compassion is developed by trying to see things from the point of view of others, and learning that their feelings are important.

Being responsible is being honest. Honesty means telling the truth. It does not mean misleading others for our own benefit. It does mean trying to make decisions, especially important ones, on the basis of evidence rather than prejudice. Honesty includes dealing with other people and being honest with ourselves. To understand the importance of being truthful to others, we need to learn that living together depends on trust. Without honesty, trusting each other becomes impossible. Honesty with ourselves involves facing up to our own mistakes and biases, even when we have to admit them to others. It includes self-criticism. The point is to learn from our mistakes, try to correct them, and move forward.

Accepting responsibility takes courage and then taking a position and doing what is right, even at the risk of some loss. It does NOT mean acting reckless or cowardly, but facing up to our duties and obligations. It includes physical courage, intellectual courage, and moral courage to stand up for our principles.

Responsible people have self-respect. They care for others. They display appropriate behavior. They refuse to put others down. They have learned that responsibility develops a good conscience to help guide them. They have learned to respect themselves and others. Similarly, they do NOT manipulate others. They have patience and tolerance for other people.

To be responsible does not come easy. It is an acquired habit that takes time. Acting responsibly is learning to feel, think, speak, and proceed with respect for ourselves and for other people. We learn to pursue our own well-being, while also being considerate of the needs and feelings of others.

It is easier to train children than to repair adults. Proper attitudes and behavior should be learned early. It is better to learn responsibility when we are young, rather than when we are older...because then, we have to change our bad habits. As we make responsible choices and stick with them, we will find that the rewards are great. Responsibility brings fairness, respect, courage, honesty, and compassion that conscientious people can share.

We are responsible for our own lives. We may not be responsible for everything that happens to us, but we are responsible for how we react to what happens to us. "Life acts. We react." Our reaction is under our control. In any life situation we are always responsible for at least one thing. We are always responsible for the attitude towards the situation in which we find ourselves. Our attitude is our reaction to what life hands us. We can be either positive or negative.

Tommy Franks, Ph.D. cannot blame anyone for his failures except himself. He cannot blame his wonderful wife, beautiful children, the baker, the butcher, or the candlestick maker. Tommy Franks, Ph.D. can only blame himself for his own shortcomings. Yes, unfortunate circumstances do come our way in life. SWSWSW. What does this mean? Some will. Some won't. So what. Some people will honor the "Golden Rule" and treat you with dignity and respect. Others won't. So what! Life is not fair. This is something that I had to learn early in life. People will do you wrong at times. People will lie to you. People will gossip about you. People will call you names. Welcome to Planet Earth. Everybody has been done wrong at one time or another. Period! We can have a pity party about it or we can be responsible and use the situation as a stepping stone to higher ground. That's our decision. Let us choose to move forward. Let us continue to aim high.

YOU CAN DO IT
By Tommy Franks, Ph.D.

Don't you dare say, "I can't". You can do it!
Never give up. You can do it!
Remember the good times you've had. You can do it!
Don't worry about the small stuff. You can do it!
Life can be so beautiful. Why? Because you are in it!
Especially now...because excitement is in the air!
Life is too short to be sad, uneventful, and boring.
A lovely rainbow always comes after the rain. The sun
     follows.
Therefore, when you feel like you are defeated,
Think positive. You can do it!
Be persistent. Be tough. Don't you dare give up!
You can be successful. It's up to you. Yes, you can do
     it!

chapter

ELEVEN

NEVER GIVE UP

As you follow your dream, never give up. You can make it. You can do it. Galileo, the Italian physicist and astronomer, had some weird ideas for his day. He believed that different objects fell at the rate of 32 Feet Per Second because of the law of gravity. He also believed that the earth was round and revolved around the sun. This type of radical thinking in the 17th Century got him into a lot of trouble. They put him in jail for this type of nonsensical thinking. Who would be so bold as to defy the status quo? Didn't everyone KNOW that the earth was flat and that the earth was the center of the universe with all the other planets revolving around it? Who would dare to be so arrogant in the 15th century to believe that the earth was round?

After being in jail for awhile, the Church and political leaders of his day decided to let him out. They thought Galileo had learned his lesson. But Galileo knew that he had discovered something that would ultimately change the world. Without the radical thinking of Galileo, there would be no space program today. There would be no aircraft, no satellites, no weather instruments, and no weather reports. Even though they threw him in jail, ridiculed him, and mocked him, Galileo followed his dream and NEVER gave up!

You have all heard "fish" stories, but I want to tell you a "crab" story. That's right...a story about a blue crab who we will name "Jimmy". Blue crabs are harvested by using a trap known as a "crab pot". The crab pot is usually made out of wire mesh. The trap contains an entrance for the crabs, but normally prohibits exit. Research has indicated that blue crabs stay together...come hell or high water.

One day, Jimmy was caught in one of these traps with several other blue crabs. Eventually, Jimmy looked around for a way of escape. He looked up and saw that there was no wire mesh at the top of the trap. He decided to go for it; however, the other nineteen crabs decided that Jimmy was staying with them because they had already decided that there was no escape. He ignored their advice and started up the side of the trap. The other crabs caught him and brought him back down to the bottom of the crab pot and told him not to try that again or else. They re-emphasized that there was no way out.

Jimmy waited several hours and then quietly took off up the other side of the trap toward the open top. The other crabs took off after him...caught him...fought with him and cut off one of his crab claws. They told him there was no way of escape from the trap...and if he attempted to escape again, they would take off the other claw.

Jimmy licked his wounds and laid low for a while. He did not want to end up as a crab cake for someone's dinner. He waited until most of the other crabs were in the far corner of the wire mess trap. Then, he made his move. Even though he only had one claw, Jimmy took off like a bullet toward the wide-open top. He almost made it, but they caught him. They fought with him repeatedly...and eventually cut off his other claw.

They said, "Jimmy, we have you now. You will have to stay with us now because you have no claws. We are sorry that you wouldn't listen, but as we told you, there is no way to get out of this trap."

Jimmy replied, "There is no wire mesh on top of this crab pot. It's all open. We can all escape. If we don't, we will be crab cakes by tomorrow evening."

One of the larger crabs spoke up and said, "Jimmy, we know what's best for everyone. No crab has ever escaped from one of these traps. We must all stick together. Now, get some sleep."

Jimmy waited until he thought they were all asleep. It was very dark, but he knew that he had to make his move now. He began to move very slowly up the side of the trap. He would go a few inches and then stop and look around to insure that no one was after him. He continued to move and then stop and then move some more...getting closer and closer to the top where freedom was awaiting. He finally made it within two inches from freedom when all of a sudden...the biggest and meanest crab...one of the nineteen...grabbed him with both claws and dragged him all the way down to the bottom of the trap again.

The crabs all responded, "We told you, but you wouldn't listen. Where did you come up with such a crazy idea that you could escape from this trap? What gave you the idea that there is no wire mesh at the top? Don't you think that we would have known it...if that was the case? Why did you not obey us and stay put? Blue Crabs always stick together...no matter what."

Later, they killed Jimmy because they said he was too radical, extreme, and rebellious. Who ever heard of a crab trap having no top? Of course, Jimmy was right. The trap had no top. He died for his faith, belief, and conviction. What happened to the other nineteen Blue Crabs? They were eaten at a crab feast in Maryland.

So what is the moral of the story? Sometimes...actually most of the time, the crowd is wrong. People said that automobiles (horseless carriages) would never replace the horse. People thought that Orville and Wilbur Wright were nuts trying to fly a machine with wings. Others said that Thomas Alva Edison was a looney tune trying to make a light bulb. Didn't he know that no one had ever done that before?

So what about you today? Are you up to the challenge of going against the status quo...the run of the mill mediocrity...following the crowd? Remember: To be a leader, thinking positive and thinking radical at times is part of the responsibility and challenge of being on the cutting edge. Basically, we as human beings DO NOT like change. We like things the way they are now...even if they can be improved upon or more efficient. We are safe in NOT rocking the boat. Peter was safe and secure while in the boat with the other eleven. He did not have to walk on the Word of Jesus and the physical water of the Sea of Galilee. But he did. That story has been written into the chronicles of history forever!

Peter was a leader. Galileo was a leader. Martin Luther King was a tremendous leader. Winston Churchill was a great leader. I believe you, too, can become another GREAT leader in our time. You have a Dream, Divine Destiny and Purpose! You are a person of greatness, compassion, love, and prominence. NEVER GIVE UP! You can make it happen...and happen well.

You are God's lily. YOU are not alone. God is with you. You are one of God's Lilies growing in His flower garden. God loves Lilies because they are productive and beautiful. They come back year after year even after the long cold winter of adverse weather. They rise above the ground and blow freely in the gentle breeze with the warm sunshine upon their heads. Lilies are the first to bloom in early spring. Lilies are flowers of character. In short, they are strong. They have an abundance of STRENGTH. They do not wilt or fall down when the tempest comes. They brave the storm and ride it out like an eagle rides out a hurricane.

Do not fear failure. Failures will happen. Failure is one of the keys to SUCCESS. It is impossible to succeed without failing. As a child, you fell many times while learning to walk. It's part of life. All GREAT SUCCESS is preceded by GREAT FAILURE. We must be willing to fail or fall on our face. Every great man/woman on planet earth has failed. The important thing is to learn from our failures. Great success is normally just one tiny step beyond our greatest failure.

Thomas Alva Edison was considered the greatest failure ever in the history of inventions. He failed more times and lost more money in experiments than any other inventor in the world. Mr. Edison failed over 10,000 times with the light bulb invention. However, he is now considered the greatest inventor in the world with 1,097 patents to his credit. His inventions have made billions and billions of dollars. Many of his colleagues said that he was out of his mind...nuts. They also said that there was absolutely no future in the electric light. Thomas Edison followed his dream. He never gave up. He proved them wrong, didn't he?

Why do things sometimes go wrong? Sometimes, bad things happen to good people.

You have read some of this earlier, but I want to tell you the full story of a loser that was a winner in disguise: This guy was the chief "loser" of the universe. He was an old gentleman...now 88 years old. His father had died when he was five. He quit school at the age of 16. By the time he was 17, he had lost four jobs. He was married at 18 and became a father by the time he was 19. At 20, his wife left him and took their baby daughter with her. At 22, he was working as a railroad conductor, but failed miserably at that job too. He later tried to join the Army, but they kicked him out. Finally, he became a farmer and again failed. He applied for law school and was rejected. He became an insurance salesman and failed. This man...it seemed, could do nothing right! Eventually, he became a cook and dishwasher in a little cafe.

He worked long hours and thought a lot about his wife and daughter. He grieved for them and begged his wife to return, but she refused. So he formulated a plan to kidnap his daughter. He waited outside in the bushes for seven days just waiting for the right time. The day came for him to execute his plan; however, that was the one day that she did not come outside. He even FAILED at committing a crime. He was the ultimate loser.

As time went on, he eventually convinced his wife to return home. They both worked in the tiny little restaurant cooking and washing dishes until he retired at the age of 65. He went to the Post Office and picked up his first social security check for the amount of $105.00. He went home feeling dejected, discouraged, and completely worthless.

However, the chief loser soon came up with another plan: He would commit suicide. This old man went outside behind his house with a pencil and piece of paper to write his "last will and testament" prior to putting his last plan into action. While he was writing, he asked himself a question? What can I do? I have failed at everything. He thought, "I can cook. I have spent most of my life behind a hot stove. I can cook."

He then went to the bank and borrowed $87.00. He bought some empty boxes and several chickens; returned home and cooked the chickens with his special little recipe in which he had perfected over the years. He began selling chicken door to door in his hometown of Corbin, KY. The rest is history. At 65, he was a washed-out failure headed for the poor house. At the age of 88 this Kentucky Colonel was a multi-millionaire that could buy anything in the whole world. Even today, Kentucky Fried Chicken is still going strong. If you don't believe me, buy some. It's not over until it's over...and the sweet slim lady has sung. So, what's the secret? Never give up! Colonel Sanders never gave up. He developed his dream and followed it.

Another time in history, a great war was going on... called the Boers War in which England had lost many of her military leaders. This war was fought in South Africa between Great Britain and the Dutch colonists (1899-1902). A young military officer returned to England after the war and was honored as a brave and selfless war hero. The people came from miles around to see this heroic and bold soldier. By the time he was 42, he was appointed as the Minister of the Royal Navy, a position that is normally held by British royalty.

After being assigned to this prestigious and prominent position for only a short year, he committed an enormous military blunder, an error in judgment. Consequently, it was blown out of proportion by the media. The people then rejected him. He became an unknown...a "washed up has been"...a man who was growing old fast. Isn't it "funny" how one day...you are the best thing since jellybeans...and the next, you are the worst dustball that ever existed? Am I right or wrong?

This man lived in obscurity and loneliness for the next 21 years. Had he merely become a mere footnote on the sands of time? Now, at 65 years old, how could he possibly do anything worthwhile for mankind? Inside his wallet was a yellow stained piece of paper that said, "I shall study, I shall learn, and one day my time will come."

Many times he would say, "I have a dream. I have a vision. I will not die a failure. I have a goal to be somebody...to serve my country in a greater way, even though currently my country has rejected me." He never lost sight of that goal. He was knocked down, but not defeated. He had been humiliated, but was not a failure.

Therefore, at the age of 65, the King of England called him back into service to serve his majesty and all of Great Britain. After five years of service, he became a household word all over the world. People would come from the east, west, north, and south to seek his wisdom and advice. He was no longer a "dust ball". Victory had become ever so SWEET to him. His dream was being fulfilled.

Years later at the famous and prestigious Eton College, he addressed the young, keen, and technical minds who were eagerly awaiting some great fanciful wisdom from this heroic icon. With his Boer hat in one hand and his cane in another, he walked slowly to the podium. Everyone was sitting with great anticipation. With an old stogy cigar between his teeth, he proclaimed these historical and famous words, "NEVER, NEVER, NEVER, NEVER, NEVER GIVE UP!" Then he left the stage. That's all he said. Dreams and goals are so important to us today. Sir Winston Leonard Spencer Churchill (1874-1965), British Statesman, author, Prime Minister, and Nobel Prize winner (1953)...never gave up. He followed his dream.

Winners keep on going in good times, bad times, sad times, hard times, and stormy times. Adversity becomes a challenge. The only thing that can stop you from being a winner is you! Winners are not born. They are made. They come in all shapes and sizes...all kinds of packages...small, large, short, tall, black, white, brown, red, and yellow. Experience, education, intelligence, money, and talent are not prerequisites. Winning is a deliberate decision. It comes from the inside out. As human beings, we are born to win; however, a decision must be made to be a winner. That decision can come early in life or late in life. The Kentucky Colonel of Kentucky Fried Chicken made that decision in his mid sixties. He decided that he would become a winner with what he had in his hands...a recipe for delicious, golden fried chicken. The world has never been the same.

Winston Churchill decided to be a winner. The difference between a loser and a winner is "a will to win" and "a determination to win" regardless of how long it takes. Victory and defeat are sometimes only seconds, minutes, or a few days apart. The turtle continued in the race. No one really expected him to win against the swift rabbit, but he did. He persevered. He continued against all odds. He never gave up! He had a winner's attitude and...a big heart. He kept on going and won.

chapter

TWELVE

Winners Are Givers

As you follow your dream, be a giver. George Washington Carver was born a SLAVE about 1860 on a farm in Missouri. His mother and father (Mary and Giles) were owned by slave owners. Mary was owned by Moses and Susan Carver (German immigrants). Giles was owned by James Grant. Shortly after young George was born, his father died. Later, he and his mother Mary were kidnapped by night raiders. ONLY young George was recovered when Moses Carver gave a $300 race horse as a ransom to get him back. George was a slave until slavery was abolished in 1865.

In his early life, he lived in a one room cabin. He walked eight miles (one-way) to attend school. He graduated from High School in Minneapolis, KS. Later, as a young adult, he was in poor health and for several years wandered around homeless doing odd jobs such as, household and yard work. Later, he became an artist, a singer, and an organist. He studied constantly.

George applied to Highland University and was accepted. This was good news. However, when he showed up for his first day of college, the principal told him to go away because he was black. What a disappointment! However, George was not discouraged.

George drifted for four more years in a homeless condition. In 1890, he entered Simpson College in Iowa. Later, in 1894 he became the first black to graduate from Iowa State College (BS in Agricultural Science) and in 1896, George received his Master's Degree. He became their first black faculty staff member. George wanted to give something back to society because George was a giver.

Finally, George was asked by Booker T. Washington to join his staff at the Tuskegee Institute in Alabama. He accepted and became the head of their Agriculture Department. George wanted to help the southern farmers with soil conservation and crop improvement. He discovered 300 different products from the peanut, such as, cheese, milk, coffee, flour, ink, dyes, plastics, wood stains, soap, linoleum, medicine oils, cosmetics, and Worcestershire Sauce. He also discovered 118 products from the sweet potato, such as, vinegar, molasses, rubber, ink, alcohol, and postage stamp glue.

By 1919 George had catapulted the peanut industry into an $80 Million a year business. Previously, peanuts were not even recognized as a crop. Peanuts were something you fed to farm animals and elephants.

President FDR gave George the Roosevelt medal in 1939. Mr. Carver received honorary doctorate degrees from Simpson College and the University of Rochester. In 1944, Congress passed a law designating 5 JAN of each year as George Washington Carver Day.

Jesus was a Giver. The price for our forgiveness of sins has been paid in full. Jesus paid our bills in full. Jesus has always been a Giver. In God's Kingdom, everything He controls…gives. The apple tree gives apples. The oak tree gives acorns. The strawberry plant gives strawberries. The mountain spring gives water. Every true Christian that God controls…gives. Period. If we are truly controlled by the Holy Spirit, we too, will be givers. And givers never lose. A success-ful person does more than just talk. He also demonstrates his actions through love. LOVE always means giving.

Laws of God are for our welfare. There is a law of giving that is absolute. "For the law of the Spirit of Life in Christ Jesus (the law of our new being), has freed me from the law of sin and death" (Amp. Rom. 8:2). "It is the Spirit that quick-ens; the flesh profits nothing: the words that I speak to you are spirit and life" (Jn.6:32). The Word of God gives us life.

Jesus said to give (Lk.6:38). He said to give first. THEN… "it shall be given unto you good MEASURE." What was Jesus actually saying? "Your gift will return to you in full and over-flowing measure, pressed down, shaken together to make room for more and running over" (Living Bible Lk.6:38). In other words, you will have more than enough.

Because of His mercy, we are very Special. In accor-dance with God's Word, we are the Apple of God's eye.

Mercy follows us around everywhere we go. Mercy brings us the LOVE of God forever. Mercy protects us from the enemy.

As a giver and leader, you will be criticized...unjustly most of the time. That is part of being a true leader. When you are a leader, you are open game for criticism. You will position yourself between the judgments of God and the mercy of God. God likes this because He, Himself, is a merciful God who will abundantly pardon. Forgiveness is part of His character. Mercy and Grace will follow.

As a leader, you will find a way to change the mind of God; i.e., Moses. The leader will intervene when judgment is at the door. God will change His mind again and again through a true spiritual leader. Will the leader make mistakes? Absolutely! That is why he or she is a leader because he learns from others as well as his own mistakes. This is part of leadership. None of us is perfect.

Remember, the leader (sent from God) has a mission to bring imperfect individuals to the precious promises of God. The leader will see it through to fulfillment. Yes, there will be setbacks and obstacles; i.e., Moses. But the promises of God will prevail. Sometimes, the wonderful God Whom we serve wants to deliver judgment to certain rebellious individuals; i.e., the golden calf people. However, God's nature is such that He would really rather have mercy and grace upon them...If He could only find a leader to intervene for them.

Sometimes, a leader will be despitefully used by the very ones that he is trying to help. Many times, he will be misunderstood by fellow soldiers of the Cross. Sometimes, a true leader will even get angry; however, he will find a way to allow God's love to shine through him even during these moments. The leader will persevere to the fulfillment of God's promises. The leader knows his purpose, dream, mission, assignment, goals, and destiny. He will change the mind of God (Ex.32:14) several times throughout his journey on Planet Earth.

The spiritual leader not only knows the Word, but he lives it. It has become a part of him. It feeds him and gives him fresh life and anointing. God speaks to the leader as He did to Jeremiah (Jer.5:1) and says, "My son, I am seeking you to do justice, to seek truth. Now, that I have found you, I will pardon your whole city. All I need is one man or one woman who will stand in the gap...and I will abundantly pardon your whole neighborhood, city, state, and country." This is a powerful paradigm (pattern) of God! But this is His standard and model of love and forgiveness. The true spiritual leader sent by God...understands this and lives it.

A true leader is NOT a candy or chocolate soldier who melts under pressure. Years ago, I did a series of articles on "The Chocolate Soldier" on one of my radio programs. Since then, many people have commented on this topic. Personally, I believe that every Christian is a soldier of some type...whether we like it or not. When we joined the Lord's Army, we became genuine soldiers of the cross...not chocolate soldiers that melt in a crisis.

In Christianity today, every TRUE soldier is a hero. If you are a soldier without heroism, you are a Chocolate Soldier Christian. During peace, true soldiers are NOT happy because they get bored and frustrated. They thrive in war. War gives them liberty and freedom. Being in the heat of the battle gives the combat war-fighter life and breath. Peace turns him into mush. War gives him heart, strength, life, energy, and vitality. Every true soldier of Christ is a hero... without exception. We are at war today with the enemy. He wants you dead. God wants you alive.

The Chocolate Soldier melts under the heat of the battle like a Hershey Bar. He is soft and is not accustomed to hardship, disease, hunger, danger, war, or death. He is a Chocolate Soldier Christian. He is used to the sweet life of pleasures, sugar, candy, and milk chocolate. He allows others to fight his battles for him. In reality, he has become far too soft to be any good in the Lord's Army. He will melt at the very smell of gunfire or tank maneuvers. He is not acquainted with the battlefield. He is fearful. He does not follow orders very well because he does not like to take orders from others. He is rebellious and likes to do his own thing. He is an unruly soldier and will either melt under fire or get himself killed in battle.

The Chocolate Soldier Christian likes to be in his own world of superficial peace. The thought of war makes him violently sick. If he hears the trumpet call to battle, he becomes paralyzed with fear.

I must tell you this. God has never made a Chocolate Soldier. Most of you have read the story of the three Hebrew children who wouldn't bow, wouldn't bend, and wouldn't burn. They were heroes and certainly not chocolate soldiers. They were accused by the Chaldeans of not bowing down and worshipping the golden image. Their accusations were accurate and true. Shadrach, Meshach, and Abednego would not bow down to the image that Nebuchadnezzar the king had set up (Dan.3).

These three true soldiers were told...that unless they fell down and worshipped this stupid, dumb, golden image, they would be cast into the fiery furnace. When they refused to bow, Nebuchadnezzar flew into a rage. He went bananas and cast the three children (heroes) into the fiery furnace. The fire was so hot that it melted the king's chocolate soldiers who threw them into the furnace. All that was left of them was chocolate syrup!

Then Nebuchadnezzar the king asked, "Didn't we cast three men bound into the fire?" They replied, "Yes, O king, that is true. Yes, Yes, we did."

The king answered, "But I see four men down there... loose, walking around in the middle of the fire. They are not melting. They are not chocolate. They are for real. They look like true soldiers. And the fourth soldier looks like the Son of God."

Finally, Nebuchadnezzar came to the edge of the fiery furnace and said, "All right, you servants of the most high God, come up here. You are indeed real soldiers...and not candy soldiers...not chocolate soldiers like the ones who threw you into the furnace."

Shadrach, Meshach, and Abednego came forth. Even though this was perhaps one of the hottest fires ever, they were not harmed in any way. They didn't melt. They didn't burn. Their hair was not singed. They did not even have the smell of smoke on their clothes or bodies.

The king spoke..."These men are blessed of God. They trusted in their God. They were delivered by their God. Therefore, I make this decree: Every people, nation, and language, which speak any thing against the God of Shadrach, Meshach, and Abednego...shall be cut in pieces, and their houses shall be made a dunghill...because there is no other God..."

The king then promoted these true heroes (soldiers) who would not bow, bend, burn, or melt. In a word, they were not chocolate soldier Christians. Not a grain of creamy chocolate, white chocolate, dark chocolate, or semi-sweet chocolate was found in them! They were solid soldiers who had weathered the storm (battle).

Therefore, let us go forth charged up with the energy of God and allow the Son of God (Jesus Christ, the Lion of Judah) to make us true heroes and true leaders of the faith. Let us refuse to be chocolate caramels in the sugar chocolate brigade of pleasure, sin, saturated fat, and hot fudge calories. The Bible says, "Therefore endure hardness, as a good soldier of Jesus Christ" (2Tim.2:3). Being a good soldier of the cross will require self-denial, honor, respect, and obedience to those over us in the Lord, and a will to fight and follow the King (Jesus).

TRUE SPIRITUAL LEADERSHIP is the ability of one person to influence another. It has little to do with what you do, but it's a matter of who you are as an individual. In other words, finding out who you are…then becoming the person that you were made to be. There are people that do great things, but they are not leaders. It is the ability to find out where you are going and then inspire others to go with you.

Leaders are not only givers of their time, talent, and treasure, but they also accept full responsibility for their decisions. They continue to bring forth and develop the potential in others through confidence, trust, and character. GREAT leaders desire to give and serve…Leadership is a by-product of that servitude.

Billions of dollars are spent annually on "want-a-be" leaders. Many of them are complete nincompoops as far as leadership. They know nothing about leadership. Why? Because leadership courses can only teach skills, not character, dreams, or vision. Leaders are made through character and vision. They are products of initiative, drive, wanting to serve mankind, trust, courage, and goals. Leaders are not born. They are developed…many times through adversity, disappointment, the challenges of life, and a need to serve…in order to make life easier for others.

A true leader is an original…not a copy. Everyone can be a leader if she chooses to be. "If it's to be…It's up to me".

Effective Leadership makes life increasingly more successful. Effective Leadership is not necessarily doing things right; however, it is doing the right thing. For example: Let's say, one day, I ask my son Thomas II to wash my car while I am away in the big city of Atlanta. However, he decides to mow the lawn instead. Upon my return, the lawn looks superb and beautiful. It is simply wonderful to gaze upon… freshly manicured; the sidewalk looks well trimmed; the plants and young trees look so good in the freshly mowed lawn. It took Thomas a lot of time to mow the lawn. He had done a good thing and he had done it right; nonetheless, he had not done the right thing. As his father, I had asked him to wash my car, not mow the lawn. My car still needed to be washed.

Another thing, the real purpose of leadership is not followers, but to lead others into becoming leaders themselves. The ultimate goal of leadership is independence and the development of more leaders.

Everyone is born to lead; however, most people die without ever knowing what they were born to do, what their purpose in life was all about, without knowing who they were, and without knowing true victory and great accomplishments. Many of them have never had a dream. WHY? They did not DARE to be themselves. They tried to be what others told them to be. They did not even attempt to achieve their goals or dreams…because they had none. They tried to be a copy and not an original.

A winner is above all things...a giver.

Winners are leaders. They inspire others. Inspiration is the direct opposite of intimidation, manipulation, or domination. To motivate another human being is one of the greatest achievements in life. Leaders will draw the best out of others and inspire them to maximize their true potential, talents, gifts, dreams, and abilities.

Everyone has the capacity, potential, and raw material to become a great leader by the design of the Creator. However, most people on Planet Earth will die with the leader trapped within them in the grave of a follower. Most people die without ever knowing who they really are. Why? Because most individuals are products of their mere environment, lacking courage to change, refusing to develop their potential, failing to maximize their gifts, and rejecting who their Master created them to be. This is a tragedy. You and I and millions of others were born to win and to be leaders. We lead. We win.

Let us not become an endangered species or extinct. God made us to be leaders. Let's do it with integrity, vigor, passion, enthusiasm, zeal, and humility. Leadership is ordained by God and usually comes unsought. The person who is faithful is the person who is granted leadership ability. We can only lead others as far as we have gone ourselves. Great leaders are ordinary people who do extraordinary things because circumstances make demands upon them and their potential.

A leader is an innovator. She does things that other people refuse to do or...do not want to do. She makes old things new. Her goal is never to become a great leader. Her goal is to serve and maximize herself in helping others. Leaders are NOT smarter than other people. They are NOT wiser than others. They are not gifted more than other people; however, they are highly motivated with a sense of purpose, passion, and sense of destiny.

A leader is calm in a crisis and resilient in adversity. As weather shapes a mountain, problems and adversities make great leaders. Leaders will control their anger. ALL LEADERS will be criticized. Period! If you are a leader, you will be criticized. Hopefully, you will step forward and be counted as the man or woman that God has called you to be. As a leader and winner, you will become a target for criticism. And remember, a true leader does not follow the crowd. The crowd follows her. WHY? Because she knows where she is going. She knows what's ahead around the bend. She has been there before.

People will follow someone who knows where he is going. The rule is: LEAD, follow, or get out of the way...or stick your head in the sand and make believe that you are an ostrich. Today, decide to LEAD as you were born to do!

As a leader, never be guilty of nursing resentments or un-forgiveness. It will kill you and damage those around you. Remember Joseph? He forgave his brothers and even saved their lives from hunger. We do not have time as leaders to harbor resentment. We must decipher the person's behavior from his potential and self-worth. Just remember, feelings, opinions, and perceptions are NOT facts. That's why we cannot afford to carry grudges against another person.

Keep your vision before you. Pamper your dreams, not wrong doings by others. Be optimistic. Try to believe that people will change. Even if they don't, continue to believe that every human being on this planet has potential and has been given talents and abilities.

Above all, be RESPONSIBLE! Stand up and be counted. Get excited about what you are doing. If you are digging a ditch, get excited about it. If you are building a house, get excited. If you are helping others, get excited about it. Expect great things to happen to you and for you and on your behalf. And they will...Winners are leaders. Winners are givers!

MERCY

By Tommy Franks, Ph.D.

Mercy rearranged my life.
Mercy took away so much of my strife.
Mercy rewrote my name.
Mercy took away the blame.
Mercy saved my life from hell.
Mercy made me whole and well.

Mercy gave me back my dignity.
Mercy enriched my life significantly.
Mercy, mercy, mercy gave me love
That could only be known from above.
Mercy brought me peace, love, and cheer
That will stand the test throughout the years.

Mercy brings compassion, forgiveness, and kindness.
Mercy brings light instead of blindness.
Mercy eradicates ignorance and brings understanding.
Mercy brings a soft heart that is less demanding.
Mercy gives and brings goodwill.
Mercy is the good life with a thrill.

Mercy rearranged my life.
Mercy took away all my strife.
Mercy wrote my name above.
Mercy and love go together like a glove.
Where would you and I be without mercy and grace?
We would be hopelessly lost in the big rat race!

chapter

THIRTEEN

Play to Win

We can still play to win even when common sense or "all odds" are against us. Some will tell us that we no longer have a chance in a million to make it happen. Even when things have not been going as planned, we can still WIN. Sure, sometimes the breaks seem to go the other way, but life is NOT against you or me. Life is for us. We can determine in our hearts and minds to approach each new day, each new adventure, and each new opportunity as a glorious gift of golden potential.

When we make things happen for others, things will happen for us. It is an unwritten rule. It is impossible to help another human being without helping ourselves. After all, we all came from Adam and Eve, did we not? Therefore, when I help another person, I am actually helping another member of my human family that is actually related to me in some way or another.

A win/win situation is available to us every single day. We breathe. We talk. We walk. We laugh. We work. We play. We live. Life is a tremendous gift to us. When we woke up this morning, we became brand new winners living in a brand new day experiencing brand new and exciting things. Excitement is in the air. Excitement is everywhere! You are alive! I am alive! We are alive! "Ain't life great?"

Just think. Our ancestors dreamed about this present day. They worked hard and long hours (12 to 14 hours a day) for peanuts...compared to what we make in our pay- checks. I remember...as a child...having an outside well for our water supply. We had no inside plumbing. We had no television...no rotary phone (black in color)...no micro- wave...no electric coffee pot. We had no windows, only wooden shutters...no heaters, just a fireplace. Every morn- ing when my little eyes opened, my scenery was cotton fields on every side with a dirt road out front. Hello!

Don't tell me about "the good old days". We are living in the "good old days" right now. That's why we need to "play to win" every single day, especially since our forefa- thers paved the way for us. The foundation has been laid already. We are so fortunate to be living in the best of times. We have the greatest technology, the finest tools, the best people around us, tremendous resources, and a multitude of golden opportunities just waiting for us to touch, taste, feel, see, hear, and explore with every fiber and tissue of our lives! We have a WIN/WIN situation and it's one great deal. "Ain't it great?" Play to win! It is the winner's inevitable destiny.

The winner always plays to win...in school...in college... in the WORKPLACE. I heard a story one time about a little boy named Sparky. Sparky was a loser in disguise. School was miserable for Sparky. He failed almost every subject in the eighth grade. He flunked physics in high school...his grade was a zero. Sparky went on to also flunked Latin, algebra, and English. His sports participation in school was not much better; although, he did manage to make the school's golf team...However, he lost the only important match of the season. He even lost the consolation match as well.

Throughout his youth, Sparky was awkward socially. He was not liked or disliked. It's just that the other students really could care less about him. He was astonished if a classmate said hello to him outside of school hours.

No one knows how he might have done at dating because Sparky never asked a girl to go out with him...in high school. He was too afraid of being turned down.

Basically, Sparky was a loser. He knew it. His classmates knew it. Everyone knew it. So Sparky just rolled with it. He had made up his mind early in life that if things were meant to work out, they would. Otherwise, he would content himself with what appeared to be his inevitable mediocrity.

However, there is more...Sparky knew how to draw. He was proud of his drawings and artwork. Of course at the time...no one else appreciated them. In his senior year of high school, he submitted some cartoons to the editors of the yearbook. The cartoons were turned down. Despite this particular rejection, Sparky was so convinced of his illustrative ability that he decided to become a professional artist. He had confidence in himself...at least in his drawings.

After completing high school, he wrote a letter to Walt Disney Studios. He was told to send some samples of his artwork. The subject for a cartoon was suggested. Sparky drew the proposed cartoon. He spent a great deal of time on it and on all the other drawings he submitted. Finally, the reply came from Disney Studios. He had been rejected once again. Another loss for the LOSER...

Sparky suddenly decided to "play to win"...no more losing for him. He decided to write his own autobiography, but do it in cartoons. He described his childhood as a little boy loser and chronic underachiever. The cartoon character would soon become famous all over the world. Sparky, the little boy who had such a lack of success in school, in life, and with people decided to be a winner. He created the "Peanuts" comic strip and the little cartoon character we love so dearly...Charlie Brown. The artist and comic strip author succeeded in playing to win in the game of life. His real name...CHARLES SCHULZ.

In order to play to win, we must examine the Law of Sowing and Reaping. We all sow something...good, bad, or indifferent. We all reap...good, bad, or indifferent. Sometimes, we receive multiple rewards. Therefore, it pays great dividends to sow good seeds. If I sow a small mustard seed, I will reap much more than what I planted. This is the law of sowing and reaping. We will reap much more than we have sown. This law is fair. It is just.

It does NOT discriminate. This is why we need to discipline ourselves daily. If we render good service, our reward will be multiplied. If we are fair, honest, and patient with others, our reward will be multiplied back to us.

When we give more of ourselves, we receive more in return. It's the law. This is NOT always easy in the game of life. As a matter of fact, this takes great effort on our part. Anything of value requires care, concern, attention, and self-discipline. Even our thoughts require discipline.

When I sow the following seeds, I will reap a harvest of some type:
- Writing a card or letter to a friend.
- Paying my bills on time.
- Being a good motorist on the highway. (This one is tough for me!)
- Managing my time properly.
- Paying my taxes.
- Reading good books.
- Coming to work on time.

As we know, life can be very "unfair" at times. Failures happen. Sometimes, bad things happen to good people. Life is NOT fair! That's why we need to plant good seeds. The more good seeds that are planted in our lives and in society, the better our lives become. For example, the next time you are on an elevator, meet someone in the hall or in the office, compliment the individual on something; i.e., her nice dress (outfit) or his nice tie...whatever. You have now sown a seed. That seed will germinate and bring forth some type of harvest. Perhaps, you made that person's day with that compliment. She will now feel better and will probably pass on a compliment to some other person within the office.

Life is real. We are living in the "here and now". What is really important to you in life? Money, job, family, peace, things, spouse, people, future aspirations? What? What do you most often think about? Where do you want to be five years from now...ten years from now? If we sow good seeds today, we will reap good rewards tomorrow.

Living in today's world is NOT easy. It takes a lot of discipline. But never give up...never! Our incredible lives are in the tissue of every fiber and moment that we live. The way I live my life today will affect my tomorrow.

We play to win by giving to others...Sharing with others is a great way to plant seeds. Serving others will bring about a harvest. Generosity and big-heartedness bring great rewards. Giving to others starts the Law of Sowing and Reaping in motion. Giving brings about receiving. One of the greatest teachers of character is generosity. Sharing with others makes us bigger than we are. The more I pour into someone or sow into a person's life, the more life will be poured into me. This is the law. We must be concerned about people. This brings much richness into our lives. When we give, it becomes an investment that brings about a return that is multiplied back to us. When we give, everybody wins.

As we have mentioned earlier, you are SPECIAL. There is more to you than what others see on the outside. You are special to your family. You are special to your friends. The past is gone forever. Today is a brand NEW day filled with opportunities. Perseverance and determination will put you over.

We can bring the best out of people. Every person has a hidden desire to be somebody important. The SECRET is...we already are. We do not have to attempt to be. We already are. We need to bring to the surface those talents that are hidden in others. Every person on Planet Earth has at least one or more talents or special abilities. It's up to us to unlock those doors of potential. We can make the difference in another person's life. When we help push someone else to the top, life will also smile upon us and we will go to the top as well. WHY? Because we are special creations.

We play to win and succeed. We use adversity as stepping stones instead of stumbling blocks. We smile in the face of disaster. We are not nameless faces. We have talent. That is the way we were made. People aren't numbers. We are human beings with faces, names, families, goals, homes, and cares.

We have experienced pain, hurt, sorrow, and joy. We are creations that were made for a purpose, identity, destiny, acceptance, and success. Treat people good, especially yourself...and eventually good will be returned to you. It's the law. Do good to others and good will come to you. We are winners. We do not have to try to be somebody. We already are. Great and positive things will happen to you today.

LAST WORDS

You have now read *BORN TO WIN: A WINNER'S DESTINY.*
What can one man or one woman do to make the world a better place? One man/woman can change the world!

Criticism across America is everywhere. Even some Christians have said, "If God doesn't destroy America, He will have to repent to Sodom and Gomorrah."

If we are going to compare the United States to Sodom, then the church should be compared to Abraham. If we take this premise to its conclusion, we will have to add, "If the Lord does not rebuke judgmental Christians, He will have to repent to Abraham!"

What am I talking about? I am referring to the fact that when Abraham was confronted with the imminent possibility of Sodom's destruction, he did not jump on the "Destroy Sodom" bandwagon; instead, he went before the Lord and prayed for mercy to be upon the city.

Somehow, we have come to believe that non-compromising Christians must also be angry. Abraham never compromised with Sodom's depraved culture, yet he was above fleshly reaction. In fact, throughout his prayer, Abraham did not even remind the Lord of what was wrong in Sodom. He appealed, instead, to the mercy and integrity of the Lord. This was one of Abraham's most noteworthy deeds...praying for Sodom, the most perverse city in the world at that time. Grace and mercy are the best solutions to the answer.

God works with man to establish the future and, in the process of determining reality...He always prepares a merciful alternative. In other words, our urgent, redemptive prayers shoot straight through the mercy door to God's heart. This door is never shut, especially since we have a High Priest, Jesus Christ, ministering at the mercy seat in the heavenlies. It is open any time and every time we pray.

Abraham knew the love of God. They were intimate friends. Abraham, in truth, had a clear view into the heart of God based on his own experience. This interceding prophet had seen the Almighty bless, prosper, and forgive him; he pressed God's mercy toward its limits.

Abraham finally secured the Lord's promise not to destroy the city if he could find just ten righteous people there. Think about this, for herein we discover the heart of God: The Lord would spare sinful Sodom for the sake of ten godly people who dwelt within it!

Now, let us get back to the above question: What can one man or one woman do to make the world a better place? Let's start with your own community. Think about your city. Think about your church. Are there at least ten honorable people who sincerely care about your community? Are there ten good folk among you? I am sure there are.

One winner in a city or community can actually make a difference. One godly individual who cares for a city (or a family or a school or a neighborhood or a church) swings open the door for grace and mercy.

If just one man or woman refuses to give in to the intimidation of increasing wickedness, if that one person refuses to submit to hopelessness, fear or unbelief, it is enough to exact from heaven a display of God's mercy. You, my friend, can be that "one" who obtains forgiveness and mercy for your community, city, or church.

Mercy far outweighs wrath. You see, whenever a winner operates in intercessory mercy, the tender passions of Christ are unveiled in the world. The Master Teacher ever lives to make intercession for us. He is seated at the right hand of God the Father praying on our behalf. He is not eagerly waiting in heaven desiring an opportunity to destroy the world, but is praying for mercy. This is His nature.

Christ, the second person of the Trinity, is God in His mercy form. He is God loving the world, granting forgiveness to souls everywhere. He paid the price for redemption. Christ is the mercy of God satisfying the justice of God.

When God declared that man was to be made in His divine image, it is this image of Christ the Redeemer that reveals our pattern. We are to follow the mercy path set by Christ. "As He is, so also are we in this world" (1 John 4:17).

Jesus came to earth to fulfill the mercy of God. His title is Redeemer. His role is Savior. He is the Good Shepherd who lays down His life for His sheep. God calls us to be like Him. Mercy always triumphs over judgment. Mercy plays exactly into God's heart. And one man or woman who reveals Christ's heart on earth will bring mercy, grace, and truth to his or her community and city. Let us be that "one" who never ceases to cry out to God for mercy.

One man or one woman can make a difference on Planet Earth. How? By having a heart of love for people... getting involved, being committed, and caring for others. The rewards are tremendous and eternal.

We serve a Great BIG, Wonderful God. He has given you the power to win in life. You were born to win. Your destiny is Planet Heaven. God loves you. You are free. Hope is real. Hope is alive. All of us are individuals created by God Himself. Every person in our society is an influence to another person in our society...good or bad. Hence, we have a responsibility to those around us to assist them in accomplishing their dreams.

God chose you before the foundation of the world. He has accepted you. He has brought you into His eternal grace. Hopefully, this book has influenced you. Read it often. Share it with others. Remember who you are...An open book being read every single day.

Nine Things that God Has Done for you:
1. He has blessed you (Eph. 1:3).
2. He has chosen you (Eph. 1:4).
3. He has predestined you to be with Him (Eph. 1:5, 11).
4. He has made you accepted (Eph. 1:6).
5. He has redeemed you (Eph. 1:7).
6. He has abounded toward you (Eph. 1:8).
7. He has made known unto you (Eph. 1:9).
8. He has given you an inheritance (Eph. 1:11, 14).
9. He has sealed you to eternal life (Eph. 1:13).

You now have True Riches: (Eph.1)
1. Riches of His grace (Eph. 1:7)
2. Riches of the glory of the inheritance in the saints (Eph. 1:18)

3. Unreachable riches of Christ (Eph. 3:8)
4. Riches of glory (Eph. 3:16; Romans 9:23)
5. Riches of His goodness (Romans 2:4)
6. Riches of wisdom, knowledge (Romans 11:33)
7. Riches in glory (Phil. 4:19)
8. Riches of the glory of the mystery of Christ in you (Col. 1:27)
9. Riches of the full assurance and understanding of God's mystery (Col. 2:2)

I want to leave you with this poem:

The Lord of the Dance
By Tommy Franks, Ph.D.

When the world began,
I danced with joy in the morning.
I danced in the moonlight with the stars.
I even danced in the warm sunshine from afar.
I came down from heaven and danced on Planet Earth.
At Bethlehem, I had My Birth!

DANCE wherever you may be,
I am (in fact) the Lord of the Dance, said He.
I'll lead every one of you if you will follow Me.
This Jew will teach you all to Dance…and be free.
If you will only respond to My call, you will see
That you too…will DANCE and have JOY through all eternity!

I danced for the sly Scribe
And the revolting Pharisee,
But they would NOT dance
And would NOT follow Me.

I danced for the fishermen as well as James and John.
They came with Me...for their DANCE had begun!

I danced on the Sabbath. I healed the people and
    cured the lame.
The "holy" people said, "Ain't that a shame!"
They then whipped Me...stripped Me...and ripped Me
And hung Me up high to dry. Yes, they thought they
    had Me.
They stared at Me with their resentful hearts and left Me
    on the Cross to die and depart.
Little did they know that I would later dance with fire
    and a forgiving heart.

I danced on Friday even when the sky turned black.
I danced and I danced. I knew the outcome, Jack!
But let Me tell you something...It's hard to Dance with
    the devil on My back.
They buried My Body...and they thought they had Me.
But then I went to hell
And Danced on the devil's back.

Oh, that was a good dance. I thought I had died and
Gone to heaven! I continued to dance all over hell.
I danced on the heads of the little demons.
I danced on the heads of the powerless evil spirits.
I said, "Glory! This is fun. I have waited for thousands
Of years for this great moment! I am the Lord of the
    Dance!"

DANCE wherever you may be,
I am (in fact) the Lord of the Dance, said He.
I'll lead everyone of you if you will follow Me.
This Jew will teach you all to Dance...and be free.
If you will only respond to My call, you will see
That you too...will DANCE and have JOY through all
    eternity!

They thought I was gone like a dead bush or tree.
But "I AM...I said, I AM. I AM the Lord of the DANCE..."
And I will be forever FREE...
And I'll go on LOVING You, My Child so that
You too, My beautiful Bride, can be FREE to DANCE
Throughout all eternity. It is your destiny to DANCE and
    be with Me.

They cut Me down and I leaped up to heaven...
To join My Father in a "Welcome Home Dance".
I am the Life that will NOT die. I am the Lord of the
    Dance!
I'll love you and will live with you forever...But there is
    one request that I must make.
You must let me lead you in our personal Dance.
Child, can I have this dance with you?

ABOUT THE AUTHOR

Dr. Tommy Franks is an established author and inspirational speaker. His previous talk show host experience, motivational seminars, conferences, and workshops have contributed to a lot of his candor and frankness. He has been writing books and articles for over forty years. Tommy's books, materials, and motivational videos have had a global impact. Dr. Franks believes in sharing his wealth of knowledge with others as he lives each day with passion. He is married to the most beautiful green eyed blonde in the world…Karen. They make their home in Florida and have six grown, energetic, and healthy children. Tommy and Karen are gifted and talented individuals who believe that every person has dignity, purpose, worth, unlimited value, and honor. They believe that every individual is born with a Specific Purpose, Divine Assignment, and Divine Destiny. They believe that you and I were born for such a time as this and that you deserve the very BEST that life has to offer. Tommy says, "After all, you are the BEST product that our loving Father has ever produced. He created YOU for GREATNESS and God wants you to have more than enough…You are a Winner: Born to Win with a Winner's Destiny…Heaven."

Dr. Tommy Franks is an established author and inspirational speaker. His previous talk show host experience, motivational seminars, conferences, and workshops have contributed to a lot of his candor and frankness. He has been writing books and articles for decades. Tommy's books, materials, and motivational videos have had a global impact. Dr. Franks believes in sharing his wealth of knowledge with others as he lives each day with energy and passion. He is married to the most beautiful green-eyed blonde in the world.Karen. They make their home in Florida and have six grown, energetic, and healthy children. Tommy and Karen are gifted and talented individuals who believe that every person has dignity, purpose, worth, unlimited value, and honor. They believe that every individual is Born to Win with a Specific Purpose, Divine Assignment, and Divine Destiny. They believe that you and I were born for such a time as this and that you deserve the very BEST that life has to offer. Tommy says, "After all, you are the BEST product that our loving Father has ever produced. He created YOU for GREATNESS and God wants you to have more than enough.You are a Winner: Born to Win with a Winner's Destiny.Heaven."

You were born to win. You were born to succeed. Success is yours. God wants you to be a winner in this life.not a failure. You have the power within you to have anything you desire. Our loving Father owns it all and He wants to share His wealth with you. As a winner, you need to see yourself as God sees you...successful, whole, healthy, and wealthy.with more than enough.

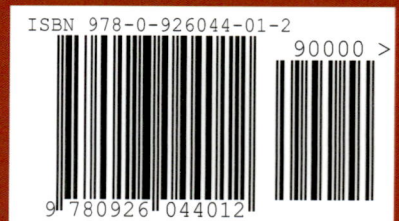

ISBN 978-0-926044-01-2

90000 >

9 780926 044012